Celebrating the Century

Andrew Mayes trained for the Anglican priesthood at King's College London – where he was awarded a First in Theology – and at St Stephen's House, Oxford. During a year at the Armenian Seminary, Jerusalem, he studied Orthodox spirituality, sponsored by the Philip Usher Memorial Scholarship. Subsequently, he studied Catholic spirituality at Heythrop College, London, and the Evangelical tradition at the Nazarene Theological College, Manchester. He was awarded a MA in Theology – with distinction – by Manchester University in 1997. He has served in parishes in London, Essex and Birmingham and is currently Vicar of St Nicholas' Church, Saltdean, Brighton. As Chairman of Sussex Churches' Renewal, he arranges and leads seminars and workshops on prayer and spiritual renewal. He is a co-author of a catechetical programme, *Following Jesus*, and a contributor to a symposium on the Oriental Orthodox Churches, *Light from the East.*

Celebrating the Christian Centuries

Andrew Mayes

For Moira,
Thank you for your
help & input
with this course,

Andrew D. Mayes

First published in Great Britain in 1999 by
SPCK, Holy Trinity Church, Marylebone Road,
London NW1 4DU

British Library Cataloguing-in-Publication Data
A catalogue record for this book is available from the British Library

ISBN 0-281-05214-X

Photoset by David Gregson Associates, Beccles, Suffolk
Printed in Great Britain by
The Cromwell Press, Trowbridge, Wiltshire

To Ann

Contents

Medieval Spiritualities: the High Middle Ages

Reformation and Renewal: into the Modern World

Introduction

THIS BOOK IS an invitation to make a journey through time. The map for our journey is an historical outline pointing out major landmark-events and developments in the experience of the Church. Our companions on the journey are outstanding Christians of the past, who will speak to us words of hope, challenge and wisdom, through texts which have inspired people down the ages. The book is a celebration of twenty centuries of Christian spirituality, offered in the hope that you will want to explore further the great writers you meet in these pages.

'Spirituality' is, of course, an all-encompassing term, once described usefully as 'the combination of praying and living'.[1] Prayer should never be divorced from witness and life in the world, so what we will be considering here are different aspects of discipleship and of Christian living. Our selection of writers aims to provide a balanced introduction to key components of Christian spirituality, and, taken together, the chapters comprise a useful and practical manual on prayer and discipleship.

The book's format means that it can be used as a course-book either by individuals or by groups. Each chapter is dedicated to one of the centuries of the Christian millennia, and begins with a short introduction to the century and to the writer chosen to represent developments in how Christians have thought about our relationship with God. Then comes a text from a primary source, from someone whose life and writings have inspired others. This is followed by questions, designed to help individuals or groups to 'unpack' the text. A choice of 'prayer exercises' provides a concluding focus and space for reflection, and, finally, some suggestions are given to encourage further reading.

Using the Course with Groups

The material in the book can be used selectively, or it may be found best to have four 'terms' with five sessions in each, as the Part headings suggest.

It would also be possible to divide the material differently, for example into three blocks each of six or seven sessions. In other words, it is intended for flexible use. In any form, it could serve as a parish celebration of the Millennium.

Those taking part in a group could be asked to read the historical introduction to each unit beforehand, and sessions could then begin with a brief look at the century, asking each time: 'What do you think it was like to live in this century?' and 'What challenges did the Christians of this age face?' This leads in to reading the information about the chosen writer. The extract itself is best read aloud, so that the text can come alive as we listen to a voice from that particular century speaking to us today.

There is no need to tackle all five questions offered in each case – each group will need to identify those most helpful to them. Group leaders may also need to look ahead at the 'prayer exercises', some of which need preparation beforehand. However, the course is designed to be a resource complete in itself, and needs little extra planning. A Bible will be useful – there are references to consider in each chapter.

Our Approach to the Past

How, then, should we approach ancient texts that come from a sometimes far-off age and thought-world? Philip Sheldrake suggests a two-way conversation: 'What is needed is a receptive and at the same time critical dialogue with a spiritual text in order to allow the wisdom contained in it to challenge us and yet to accord our own horizons their proper place.'[2] My hope is that this book will enable us to talk and interact with Christians of the past, inspiring our spiritual journey and witness, as God leads us forward into his future.

NOTES

1. G. Wainwright, 'Types of Spirituality' in C. Jones, G. Wainwright and E. Yarnold (eds), *The Study of Spirituality* (SPCK, London, 1986), p. 592.
2. P. Sheldrake, *Spirituality and History* (SPCK, London, 1991), p. 165.

Beginnings:
the Early Church

The 1st Century:
Clement of Rome

THE FIRST CENTURY saw the beginning of a movement that was to change the world. In the years after the first Pentecost, the words of Jesus to the first disciples began to find fulfilment: 'You shall receive power when the Holy Spirit has come upon you; and you will be my witnesses in Jerusalem, and in all Judea and Samaria, and to the end of the earth' (Acts 1.8). Fuelled by the Spirit, the first Christians were described as 'men who have turned the world upside down' (Acts 17.6) by their paradoxical message of a God in human flesh bringing salvation through death on a cross, and a new kind of life made possible by the risen Christ.

The early evangelists established small communities of Christians who welcomed believers through baptism and found nourishment through the breaking of bread – the eucharist. The growing churches were marked by a sharing of gifts both material and spiritual (Acts 2.43–7), by a quality of fellowship and a keen sense of belonging and participation. Radically, there was a breaking down of barriers that had kept people apart for centuries: 'There is neither Jew nor Greek, there is neither slave nor free, there is neither male nor female; for you are all one in Christ Jesus' (Galatians 3.28). Their spirituality was based on a pondering of the Old Testament Scriptures in the light of the resurrection of Christ.

The first century can be characterized by a search for identity: a gradual and sometimes painful separation from Judaism and the synagogue. It was at Antioch that the disciples were first called 'Christians' and their priorities were mission – in the face of misunderstanding and persecution – a readiness to share resources and encouraging new ministries (see Acts 11.19–30; 13.1–3). But we must not over-glamorize these first Christian communities. They consisted of ordinary men and women stepping out together into a great new adventure – lives gradually becoming transformed but still in need of healing and discipline.

CLEMENT was Bishop of Rome at the end of the century, probably the third after Peter. We do not know a lot about him. It is possible that he was an ex-slave, a freedman belonging to the household of Flavius Clemens, a cousin of the Emperor Diocletian; he may be the Clement mentioned in Paul's letter to the Philippians (4.3), described as a 'labourer for the gospel'. Certainly Clement is revealed in his own letter as a passionate pastor, deeply anxious for the unity and peace of a sister church. Traditionally, Clement was banished from Rome by Emperor Trajan, and was martyred at the end of the century by being thrown into the sea attached to an anchor.

The *First Epistle of Clement* is one of the earliest Christian texts outside the New Testament, written to the Christians at Corinth from Rome in about AD 95. The church at Corinth consisted of a number of household gatherings, meeting throughout the cosmopolitan city, and coming together regularly in the larger house of Gaius (Romans 16.23). The divisions evident in Paul's letters had not gone away – now junior leaders were ousting the older existing ones, prompting Clement to call for deep repentance. In his letter, he refers to the martyrdom of Peter and Paul as having already taken place in Rome, and gives us clues to understand an emerging Christian spirituality. He stresses that faith is evidenced by good works, and humility and love must be the chief Christian attitudes.

A Reading from Clement of Rome

The all-merciful and beneficent Father is compassionate to those that fear Him; to approach Him in sincerity of heart is to be repaid with His kind and gracious favours. So let us be done with vacillation, and indulge no more inward doubts of the reality of his great and glorious gifts [. . .] Think, my dear friends, how the Lord offers us proof after proof that there is going to be a resurrection, of which He has made Jesus Christ the first-fruits by raising Him from the dead. My friends, look how regularly there are processes of resurrection going on at this very moment. The day and the night show us an example of it; for night sinks to rest, and day arises; day passes away, and night comes again. Or take the fruits of the earth; how, and in what way, does a crop come into being? When the sower goes out and drops each seed into the ground, it falls to the earth shrivelled and bare, and decays; but presently the power of the Lord's providence raises it from decay, and from that single grain a host of others spring up and yield their fruit [. . .]

'Open me the gate of righteousness, that I may go in and praise the Lord. This is the gate of the Lord; the righteous shall come in by it.' There are many gates standing open, but the 'gate of righteousness' is the gate of Christ, where blessings are in store for every incomer who pursues the path of godliness and uprightness, and goes about his duties without seeking to create trouble. By all means let a man be a true believer, let him be capable of expounding the secrets of revelation, and a judicious assessor of what he hears, and a pattern of virtue in all his doings. But the higher his reputation stands, so much the more humble-minded he ought to be; and furthermore, his eyes should be fixed on the good of the whole community rather than on his own personal advantage.

If there is true Christian love in a man, let him carry out the precepts of Christ. Who can describe the constraining power of a love for God? Its majesty and its beauty who can adequately express? No tongue can tell the heights to which love can uplift us. Love binds us fast to God. Love casts a veil over sins innumerable. There are no limits to love's endurance, no end to its patience. Love is without servility, as it is without arrogance. Love knows of no divisions, promotes no discord; all the works of love are done in perfect fellowship. It was in love that all God's chosen saints were made perfect; for without love nothing is pleasing to Him. It was in love that the Lord drew us to Himself; because of the love He bore us, our Lord Jesus Christ, at the will of God, gave His blood for us – His flesh for our flesh, His life for our lives. See then, dear friends, what a great and wondrous thing love is. Its perfection is beyond all words [. . .]

[Teach us, O Lord] to hope in thy Name, which is the source and fount of all creation. Open the eyes of our hearts to know thee, who alone art Highest amid the highest, and ever abidest Holy amidst the holy [. . .] Thou settest up the lowly on high, and the lofty thou dost cast down [. . .] Thou alone art the discerner of every spirit [. . .] Thine eyes behold the depths and survey the works of man; thou art the aid of those in peril, the saviour of them that despair, the creator and overseer of everything that hath breath. By thee the nations of the earth are increased; and from all mankind thou hast chosen out such as love thee through thy dear child Jesus Christ, by whom thou hast taught us and raised us to sanctification and honour. Grant us, O Lord, we beseech thee, thy help and protection. Do thou deliver the afflicted, pity the lowly, raise the fallen, reveal thyself to the needy, heal the sick, and bring home thy wandering people. Feed thou the hungry, ransom the captive, support the weak, comfort the faint-hearted. Let all the nations of the earth know that thou art God alone, that Jesus Christ is thy child, and that we are thy people and the sheep of thy pasture.

> From *The First Epistle to the Corinthians*, 23, 48, 49, 59,
> in M. Staniforth (tr.), *Early Christian Writings* (Penguin,
> Harmondsworth, 1968).

QUESTIONS TO PONDER

1. The first Christians were an 'Easter people' and the foundation of their faith was the resurrection: the reality of the risen Christ and the hope of new life (see 1 Corinthians 15). It must be our touchstone and starting-point too. What 'processes of resurrection' – to use Clement's words – can we identify in our own lives, what deaths and new starts? For clues, look up Colossians 3.1–17.
2. In the second paragraph, Clement mentions three aspects of being a 'true believer'. How do we measure up to these?
3. He goes on to say that 'eyes should be fixed on the good of the whole community rather than on personal advantage'. How does our individual spirituality relate to that of the local church? How can your prayer and gifts inspire others? See 1 Corinthians 12 for Paul's answer.
4. In his prayer, Clement says that Jesus Christ has 'raised us to sanctification and honour'. Our calling is holiness and a new dignity in Christ. How do you define holiness?
5. What other lines stand out from the passage? Choose one line and reflect on why it has struck you.

PRAYER EXERCISE

Either:
It is in baptism that we die to self and rise to live Christ's risen life. Place a bowl of water in front of you as a prayer-focus and reminder of the font. Slowly read Romans 6.1–11. As this course starts, let us go back to our beginnings. Take time to ponder and renew your baptismal commitment (using forms available in service books, for example for the Easter Vigil). Conclude with reading Clement's prayer.

Or:
Read slowly John 12.24: 'Truly, truly, I say to you, unless a grain of wheat falls into the earth and dies, it remains alone; but if it dies, it bears much fruit.' In a

time of silence, ask Christ to show you what in your life must die – something you must let go of, or give up. In your mind picture something beautiful growing up in its place – some new attitude or challenge. Give thanks for 'processes of resurrection' in your life.

For Further Reading

Cwiekowski, F. J., *The Beginnings of the Church*. Gill & Macmillan, Dublin, 1988.

Moyes, G., *Discovering the Young Church*. Lion, Oxford, 1989.

The 2nd Century:
Ignatius of Antioch

THE SECOND CENTURY witnessed the rapid expansion of the Christian movement: throughout North Africa, present-day Turkey, Greece, Italy and France, reaching the shores of Britain before its close.

Communications throughout the Roman empire were aided by the excellent road network and by the wide use of the Greek language, which was used by the Church for teaching and writing. At the heart of the empire was a moral bankruptcy and spiritual emptiness – contemporary philosophies and mystery religions revealing a spiritual thirst and search for meaning which the Christian message could fulfil and answer. The century was graced by the presence of able evangelists and theologians who, reflecting on the unique and astonishing doctrines of incarnation and atonement, sought to articulate a reasoned defence of the faith both for enquirers and opponents.

The clarification of Christian truth or 'orthodoxy' became vital also in the face of heretical ideas which did not do justice to the Christian revelation, and teachers engaged in lively debate with people like the Gnostics, who taught that we can get to God by acquiring secret knowledge, and the Docetists, who maintained that the divine Christ only appeared to be human, but was not really so.

Meanwhile, in hundreds of local communities, Christians still gathered in homes to worship and learn together – Christianity was still mainly an urban movement, based in the towns and cities. But Christians continued to be marginalized in society, facing ridicule, misunderstanding and downright misrepresentation. Sometimes they were accused of incest, because they were loving as brothers and sisters, and of cannibalism, because they ate 'the Body of Christ' in the eucharist. Indeed, distinctive lifestyles set Christians apart, in a sense, from the world – churches were 'counter-cultural groups', their values and priorities going against the grain of society.

Celsus, a fierce critic at the end of the second century, complained that even uneducated Christians would grasp every chance to witness to people, and were drawn to humble and poor sections of the community. Certainly, there was something deeply attractive and magnetic about these Christian fellowships. Each person was valued and discovered some form of ministry and service. Their joy and faith were contagious. And it also began to be rumoured of them: 'See how those Christians love one another.'

IGNATIUS may have been a pagan and an oppressor of Christians before his conversion. He went on to become a Christian leader of courage and determination as the second Bishop of Antioch, presiding over an increasingly important and well-organized Christian centre. But conflict with the authorities in the early years of the second century earned him the death-sentence and he was sent to Rome to face execution. He saw his journey to death as an imitation of the way to the cross and sent a message to the Roman Christians urging them not to deprive him of the privilege of martyrdom for the sake of Christ. Though he was under the guard of ten soldiers during his long overland journey, he was sometimes able to meet local Christians in the towns he passed through, and en route wrote a series of letters to churches throughout Asia Minor, to hearten them and encourage them to stand firm in their faith. These reveal him to be a clear and vigorous defender of Christ's divinity and a firm believer in the role of the bishop as guardian of the true faith. At his journey's end, it is said that Ignatius calmly faced the lions in Rome's Colosseum, in AD 107.

A Reading from Ignatius of Antioch

Regarding the rest of mankind, you should pray for them unceasingly, for we can always hope that repentance may enable them to find their way to God. Give them a chance to learn from you, or at all events from the way you act. Meet their animosity with mildness, their high words with humility, and their abuse with your prayers. But stand firm against their errors, and if they grow violent, be gentle instead of wanting to pay them back in their own coin. Let us show by our forbearance that we are their brothers, and try to imitate the Lord by seeing which of us can put up with the most ill-usage or privation or contempt – so that in this way none of the devil's noxious weeds may take root among you, but you may rest in Jesus Christ in all sanctity and discipline of body and soul.

The end of all things is near. From now onwards, then, we must bear ourselves with humility, and tremble at God's patience for fear it should turn into a judgement upon us. Let us either flee from His future wrath, or else embrace His present grace; no matter which, so long as we are found in Jesus Christ with our true life before us. Apart from Him, nothing else should have any value in your eyes; but in Him, even these chains I wear are a collar of spiritual pearls to me, in which I hope to rise again through the help of your intercessions. May there always be a place for me in those intercessions, so that I too may have part and lot among the men of Ephesus – Christians who in the power of Jesus Christ have ever been of the self-same mind as the Apostles themselves.

I know well what I am, and what you are to whom I write. I am the condemned; you are the pardoned. I am in peril; you are in security. You are the gateway, through which we are escorted by Death into the presence of God. You are initiates of the same mysteries as our saintly and renowned Paul of blessed memory (may I be found to have walked in his footsteps when I come to God!), who has remembered you in Christ Jesus in every one of his letters.

Do your best, then, to meet more often to give thanks and glory to God. When you meet frequently, the powers of Satan are confounded, and in the face of your corporate faith his maleficence crumbles. Nothing can better a state of peaceful accord, from which every trace of spiritual or earthly hostility has been banished.

Given a thorough-going faith and love for Jesus Christ, there is nothing in all this that will not be obvious to you; for life begins and ends with two qualities. Faith is the beginning, and love is the end; and the union of the two together is God. All that makes for a soul's perfection follows in their train, for nobody who professes faith will commit sin, and nobody who possesses love can feel hatred. As the tree is known by its fruits, so they who claim to belong to Christ are known by their actions; for this work of ours does not consist in just making professions, but in a faith that is both practical and lasting.

Indeed, it is better to keep quiet and be, than to make fluent professions and not be. No doubt it is a fine thing to instruct others, but only if the speaker practises what he preaches. One such Teacher there is: He who 'spake the word, and it was done'; and what He achieved even by His silences was well worthy of the Father. A man who has truly mastered the utterances of Jesus will also be able to apprehend His silence, and thus reach full spiritual maturity, so that his own words have the force of actions and his silences the significance of speech. Nothing is hidden from the Lord; even our most secret thoughts are ever present to Him. Whatever we do, then, let it be done as though He Himself were dwelling within us, we being as it were His temples and He within us as their God. For in fact, that is literally the case; and in proportion as we rightly love Him, so it will become clear to our eyes.

From *The Epistle to the Ephesians*, 10–15,
in M. Staniforth (tr.), *Early Christian Writings* (Penguin,
Harmondsworth, 1968).

QUESTIONS TO PONDER

1. Identify in this passage six or so elements of Christian living. Are these as relevant today as in the second century?
2. 'Try to imitate the Lord.' Ignatius calls his readers to an 'imitation of Christ'. In what ways is this a helpful concept for discipleship and prayer? How could the idea of copying Jesus be unhelpful, if it is taken alone as the ideal?
3. What does Ignatius teach here about the prayer of intercession? Review the scope of your intercession. What more should you include? How can our intercessions be balanced? How do you handle the idea of 'praying for the rest of mankind'?
4. What does Ignatius have to say about overcoming the evil one? Do you recognize this as an important dimension of prayer?
5. 'Apprehend His silence, and thus reach spiritual maturity'. What does Ignatius teach about the role of silence? Why is it a path to spiritual maturity? What place is given to silence in your individual and corporate prayer?

PRAYER EXERCISE

Either:
Make a large paper or cardboard cross and cut it into six irregular pieces to form a 'prayer jigsaw'. Label each piece with the elements you identified in Q.1. Slowly put the jigsaw together with three minutes' silent reflection for each piece, and as it takes the form of a cross reflect about these key dimensions of prayer and discipleship. As this course gets under way, surrender these different areas of your Christian life to God and ask for growth in each of them. Give thanks for your spiritual kinship and communion with the Christians of the second century.

Or:
Take time to be completely still. Reflect on Ignatius' intriguing references to the silences of Christ. Imagine when Jesus might have kept silent, or recall

from the Gospels moments of silence. Ask God for the grace to create silent spaces in your life, when you can listen to his voice.

FOR FURTHER READING

Barr, R., *Main Currents in Early Christian Thought*. Paulist Press, New York, 1966.

For the idea of a 'prayer jigsaw' see Mitton, M., *Saints at Prayer*. Anglican Renewal Ministries, Derby, 1994.

The 3rd Century:
Cyprian of Carthage

THE THIRD CENTURY enabled the Christian faith to advance, becoming particularly well established in parts of North Africa, with important bases at Carthage (present-day Tunisia) and at Alexandria in Egypt. The latter became a flourishing centre of spirituality and theology, where the Good News interacted creatively with the world of Greek ideas. Clement of Alexandria led a catechetical school – a sort of Christian university – where the Christian message was developed through ideas derived from Plato's philosophy. Meanwhile, in Carthage, the theologian Tertullian pioneered a contrasting type of Christian thinking, using Latin concepts. Clement and Tertullian were forerunners of different approaches to theology that were to become immensely influential.

But trouble was brewing. Up to this point, oppression of Christians had been localized, intense but sporadic. Even Britain had not escaped occasional victimizations – as early as 209 seeing its first martyr when Alban, a soldier at Verulamium, took the place of a priest and was tortured and killed during the persecutions of Septimus Severus. But now a new imperial policy demanded greater compliance. From mid-century the Emperor Decius attempted to hold a crumbling empire together by insisting on sacrifices and the burning of incense to the gods of the imperial cult – every citizen had to obtain a certificate to attest his participation in these ceremonies which were at once patriotic and idolatrous. Christians were split as to their response to the decree. Should they prove their loyalty to the Emperor or to Christ? Some dutifully conformed (going through the motions no doubt with a degree of detachment), while others resisted and faced the consequences.

CYPRIAN (200–58) was bishop in Carthage in North Africa at this time. He had been made bishop just two years after his conversion. A life centred on culture and riches – he had been a public orator and lawyer – had gained new focus and direction when, after studying the Bible and the writings of Tertullian, Cyprian embraced a lifestyle of celibacy and poverty.

Heavily criticized for fleeing Carthage during the emperor's vicious clampdown on the Christians, he returned to the city in 251 to lead the church forward once again. He began by saluting the martyrs who paid the ultimate price for their refusal to take part in the pagan rites, and the 'confessors' who were imprisoned for standing up for Jesus Christ. But what should he do with those whose nerve had crumbled, who had obtained the required certificates by compromising their faith? He allowed them back to Communion only after a period of public penance and confession. His writings reveal the dilemmas of Christians in any time of testing.

Cyprian himself was to face martyrdom when, during the persecutions of the Emperor Valerian, he refused to deny his faith or pass on the names of his clergy to the authorities.

A Reading from Cyprian

At last, dear brethren, peace has been restored to the Church and, though the pessimists thought it improbable and the pagans impossible, we have recovered our liberty through the avenging intervention of God [. . .] We must give praise to God; we must acknowledge His blessings and gifts by our thanksgivings – though in fact our lips never ceased giving thanks even in the face of persecution; for, however great be the power conceded to the Enemy against us, he can never prevent those who love God with their whole heart and soul and strength from proclaiming His blessings and hymning His praises at all times and places [. . .]

Our confessors are a joy to look upon, men whose renown is on every tongue, whose courage and faith have covered them with glory; long have we yearned after them with passionate longing, and we embrace them at last, and affectionately impress on them the sacred kiss. They form the bright army of the soldiers of Christ, whose steadfastness broke the fierce onslaught of persecution, ready as they were for the long-suffering of prison life, steeled to the endurance of death. Valiantly you repudiated the world; to God you offered a glorious spectacle, to your brethren an example to follow. Your pious lips pronounced the name of Christ and acknowledged your unchanging faith in Him; your hands, which none but sacred works had occupied, were kept unsullied by any sacrilegious sacrifice; your lips sanctified by the food of heaven, would not admit, after Our Lord's body and blood, the contamination of idolatrous sacrifices [. . .]

These heavenly crowns of the martyrs, these spiritual triumphs of the confessors, these outstanding exploits of our brethren cannot, alas, remove one cause of sorrow: that the Enemy's violence and slaughter has wrought havoc among us and has torn away something from our very heart and cast it to the ground [. . .]

At the first threatening words of the Enemy, an all too large number of the brethren betrayed their faith; they were not felled by the violence of the persecution, but fell of their own free will [. . .]

To him who prays with all his heart, to him who mourns with tears and sighs of true repentance, to him who by good works of persevering charity pleads to the Lord for mercy on his sin – to such He can extend His mercy [. . .] Nay, when a man's reparation is such to touch His heart still more, when the sincerity of his pleading appeases His anger at the offence, He equips the vanquished with arms once more, and restores and reinforces the vitality whereby faith is renewed and can bear fruit. A soldier once more he will return to the fray, he will engage anew and challenge the enemy – and will do so with all the more zest for his remorse. He who has made such satisfaction to God, he who by his repentance and shame for his sin, draws from the bitterness of his fall a fresh fund of valour and loyalty, shall by the help he has won from the Lord, rejoice the heart of the Church whom he has so lately pained; he will earn not merely God's forgiveness, but His crown.

From *Treatise on the Lapsed*, 1, 2, 4, 7, 36,
in M. Bévenot (tr.), *Ancient Christian Writers: St Cyprian* (Newman Press,
New York, 1956).

QUESTIONS TO PONDER

1. Reread the first paragraph. Recall times when you have managed to praise God in the midst of adversity. Is this what Paul means in 1 Thessalonians 5.16–18?
2. Cyprian praises the 'confessors' and 'martyrs'. The root meaning of the word 'martyr' is witness. In what ways can our life of prayer fuel and resource our Christian witness today? How can our witness become stronger if our prayer-life is growing?
3. What compromises with the world tempt today's Christian? What 'grey areas' do we face where, like the Christians of Carthage, we are not sure

how to respond as Christians? When is it particularly difficult to stand up as a Christian? How do we deny Christ today?

4. Repentance and restoration, failure and new starts: is this the heart of the gospel? What teaching of Jesus about this can you recall?

5. Look again at the two references to disciples as 'soldiers'. How useful do you find this today?

PRAYER EXERCISE

Either:
Lay out a world map before the group, and ask people to place a votive candle (night light) on places in the world where there is persecution or oppression of Christians today. Intercede for them, and for courage in your own life of witness.

Or:
Place a cross on the table. Read John 18.15–27 (Peter's denials) and reflect on times when you have failed to give clear witness. Then read John 21.15–19 (Peter's restoration) and celebrate with a song or prayer Christ's forgiveness and re-empowering.

FOR FURTHER READING

Frend, W. H. C., *Martyrdom and Persecution in the Early Church*. Blackwell and New York University Press, Oxford and New York, 1965.

The 4ᵗʰ Century:
Basil the Great

THE FOURTH CENTURY was a time of momentous change for the Christian Church. The Emperor himself, Constantine, became a Christian: in 313, his Edict at Milan proclaimed religious freedom for Christians and pagans alike, and marked the end of persecutions. The building of churches was now permitted, Constantine himself erecting basilicas at Bethlehem, Jerusalem and Rome, and he began the construction of a magnificent cathedral dedicated to 'Holy Wisdom' in Byzantium. His moving the capital of the Empire to this city, which he renamed Constantinople, had the effect of beginning a process of east/west division in both Church and Empire. However, Constantine tried to bring unity to a Church becoming deeply divided by the controversy caused by Arius, who was questioning the nature of Christ's divinity. He convened the Council of Nicaea in 325, which put together the basis of the Creed in use today. Arguments about the identity of Christ and the Trinity required ever clearer articulation of orthodox faith, and produced the outstanding theologians Athanasius, Ambrose and Gregory of Nyssa, while Jerome made the Bible more widely accessible through his Latin translation. In 380 the Emperor Theodosius declared Christianity to be the required religion throughout the Empire, cementing the marriage between Church and State. Things would never be the same again. On his death, the Empire was divided east/west between his two sons.

Monastic life developed partly as a reaction against the nominalism creeping into the Church after the persecutions ended: Christians 'in name only' content with superficial commitment to Christ. Thousands seeking to rediscover a more demanding and radical discipleship created tiny settlements in the solitude of the deserts and remote areas of Egypt, Syria, Palestine and Asia Minor. Whether living alone as hermits or together in community, these men and women pursued the same aim – to come face to face with God, without the noise of the city, without the usual barriers and distractions that can impede a relationship with God.

✠

BASIL the Great (330–79) was born in Cappadocia, the elder brother of Gregory of Nyssa. After a rich education in Constantinople and Athens, he turned his back on the world and became a monk. After visiting monasteries in Syria and Egypt, he settled at Annisi on the River Iris in Pontus (present-day Turkey), and established a number of monasteries in the region. Called to become Bishop of Caesarea in 370, he worked hard to drive out the Arian heresy and to strengthen the faith of Nicaea in a large part of Asia Minor and western Syria. His keen mind was able to see with clarity the issues involved in reaching a balanced understanding of the person of Christ.

Most of all, Basil was a man of great personal holiness and prayer. He formulated a 'Rule' to give the emerging monastic communities in Pontus a structure and an organization, guidelines to govern common life, worship and work, which were to influence St Benedict and which are still in use today in the Eastern Church. In his letters to his friend Gregory of Nazianzus, written to encourage him to join his community by the River Iris at Annisi, Basil starts to describe the aims and objectives of this lifestyle centred on prayer and mutual service.

A Reading from Basil the Great

One should aspire at keeping the mind in quietude (*hesychia*). The eye that wanders continually around, now sideways, now up and down, is unable to see distinctly what lies under it; it ought rather to apply itself firmly to the visible object if it aims at a clear vision. Likewise, the spirit of man, if it is dragged about by the world's thousand cares, has no way to attain a clear vision of the truth [. . .] Each day arrives, each in its own way obscuring the mind; and the nights, taking over the cares of the day, deceive the soul with obnoxious phantasms. There is only one escape: withdraw from the world altogether. Now this withdrawal does not mean that we should leave the world bodily, but rather break loose from the ties of 'sympathy' of the soul with the body. This means to be without a city, without a house, without anything of our own, without property, without possessions, without resources, without affairs, without con-tracts, without being taught by men, but making ready to receive in our heart the imprint of divine teaching.

The solitude offers a very great advantage for our task [. . .] Let therefore the site of the monastery be most like our place here [Annisi], free from the commerce of men, so that nothing may come from without and break the continuity of the *askesis*, for a pious *askesis* nurtures the soul with divine thoughts. Is there a greater happiness than to imitate on earth the choir of angels? At daybreak, to get up at once for prayer and honour the Creator with hymns and canticles? Then, when the sun shines with its pure light, to rush to work, to be accompanied everywhere with prayer and, so to speak, to season our labour with the salt of hymns; to establish the soul in joy and drive out sadness is the gift and the comfort of the hymns. Quietude is therefore the principle of purification of the soul, when the tongue does not speak the words of men, when the eyes do not turn all around to behold the complexion and the proportion of bodies, when the hearing does not loosen the spirit with sweet tunes composed for pleasure, or with jokes or buffoon cries most apt to unnerve the strength of the soul.

[. . .] The high road leading to the discovery of duty is the study of the inspired Scriptures. In them are found rules of action, and the lives of the blessed which the Scriptures have transmitted to us are like living images of the godly life set before us that we may imitate their good works.

[. . .] Prayers succeeding to lecture rejuvenate and invigorate the soul, which is moved toward God by desire, for beautiful is the prayer that impresses into the mind a clear notion of God. This is properly the 'inhabitation' of God, to have God seated in oneself through memory. Thus we become a temple of God, when earthly cares do not interrupt the continuity of memory, when the mind is not disturbed by unforeseen passions and when, fleeing from all things, the friend of God withdraws unto God, drives out all incitements to evil, and holds fast to those practices that lead to virtue.

From Letter 2 to Gregory Nazianzus,
in G. Barrois (tr.), *The Fathers Speak*
(St Vladimir's Seminary Press, New York, 1986).

QUESTIONS TO PONDER

1. Basil begins by talking about the need for quietude, focus and single-mindedness 'to attain a clear vision of the truth'. How do you disengage from the pressures of the day when you enter prayer? How do you deal with distractions in prayer? Noting what Basil says about the eyes, do you find a visual focus helpful or do you prefer to 'shut down' your senses?
2. What led the Desert Fathers to go to the wilderness? What place can there be for withdrawal in today's spirituality? Recall experiences of retreats,

quiet days, prayer walks. What is your experience of solitude? How can we create solitude in our working lives?

3. Basil writes 'break free from the ties of sympathy of the soul with the body'. Is this distinction between soul and body helpful – or does such a dualism undermine a more holistic approach to life? Are there 'ties of sympathy' that we need to break free from? What place is there for renunciation in today's discipleship?

4. '*Askesis* nurtures the soul with divine thoughts.' The word *askesis* means literally 'training' or 'exercise' and gives rise to the word 'asceticism'. The picture is that of a spiritual athlete (look up 1 Corinthians 9.24–7). What forms of spiritual training do we need to develop? And, if being a disciple entails disciplines, what place is there today for spiritual disciplines like fasting?

5. The aim of *askesis* is to become more fully the 'temple and inhabitation of God'. Look up the scriptural basis for this metaphor in 1 Corinthians 3.16, 17; 2 Corinthians 6.14–7.1. Do these texts ask us to separate from the world?

Prayer Exercise

Either:
Place stones in a circular tray with a central candle and dim the lights for an image of the desert. Read slowly Mark 1.12–13 (Jesus in the wilderness) and Mark 6.30–32 (his invitation to the disciples). In the stillness take stock of how much quietude there is in your life. Ask Christ to show you where you can create deserts or quiet spaces in your daily and weekly routine. End by praying Psalm 131.

Or:
Perhaps using the same initial focus, try a simple awareness exercise. Take time to relax. Listen to the different sounds outside. Then listen to yourself breathing: hear your breath! Then listen for God's 'still, small voice of calm'. Repeat slowly 'Speak Lord, your servant is listening'. Wait expectantly in the stillness, and welcome God as the Lord coming to his temple. Close the exercise by saying the Lord's Prayer slowly. If in a group, share experiences afterwards.

For Further Reading

Nouwen, H., *The Way of the Heart*. Darton, Longman & Todd, London, 1996.
Ward, B. (tr.), *The Sayings of the Desert Fathers*. Mowbray, London, 1984.

The 5th Century:
Augustine

THE FIFTH CENTURY saw the collapse of the Roman Empire in the west, overrun by successive invasions and spiralling into social chaos. In 410 the city of Rome was sacked by the Visigoths, and fell to the Vandals in 455. By 476 the empire lay in ruins, fragmenting into various barbarian kingdoms. Constantine's relocation of the capital to the east had created a massive power vacuum in the west and an absence of capable leaders and administrators. Into this gap the Church stepped forward to meet some of the most urgent needs. Responding to the breakdown in law and order in many of the towns and cities, bishops became increasingly involved in the tasks of local government and social welfare. They had the organizational skills needed to hold communities together.

What amazing changes had come to the Church within the space of a few generations! The whole character of discipleship was becoming transformed, but these changes brought both new opportunities and new risks. Out of hiding, Christians now worshipped in impressive basilicas capable of holding hundreds. Public worship enabled an unguarded proclamation of the gospel, and led to a creative development of liturgy and ceremonial. But the intimacy and support of close-knit fellowship, possible in a domestic setting, were sacrificed. Into a crumbling society Christians came forward to play their part in the rebuilding of shattered communities. But opportunities for service sometimes involved dangerous entanglements in complex politics and in local conflicts.

The papacy too took on a stronger role, its influence becoming wider. The empire continued in the east, centred on the 'New Rome' where the Patriarch of Constantinople was becoming the focus of authority for Eastern Christians.

AUGUSTINE (354–430) was completing his *Confessions* at the beginning of the century, relating the story of his conversion at Milan fourteen years earlier, where the bishop Ambrose had helped him on his journey from philosophy to faith. At the age of thirty-two, after years of searching, Augustine had surrendered his life to Christ, bringing his brilliant mind into the service of the Church. The new century found him at the city of Hippo as leading bishop of the Church in North Africa. He became a prolific writer, his theological ideas taking shape in the crucible of heated conflict with both the rigorist and exclusive Donatists and Pelagius who seemed to be undermining the gospel with an over-emphasis on man's efforts in salvation.

Augustine took forward Christian thinking in many issues, influencing the Church for centuries to come, positively through his teaching on grace, negatively with his concept of inherited original sin. In *The City of God* Augustine tried to come to terms with the fall of Rome by distinguishing the eternal church community from the transient secular society. As he lay dying in 430, ready to enter the next world, the Vandals were at the city walls of Hippo, continuing their ruthless advance.

A Reading from Augustine of Hippo

Late have I loved you, beauty so old and so new: late have I loved you. And see, you were within and I was in the external world and sought you there, and in my unlovely state I plunged into those lovely created things which you made [...] You called and cried out loud and shattered my deafness. You were radiant and resplendent, you put to flight my blindness. You were fragrant, and I drew in my breath and now pant after you. I tasted you, and I feel but hunger and thirst for you. You touched me, and I am set on fire to attain the peace which is yours.

When I shall have adhered (Psalm 72.28) to you with the whole of myself, I shall never have 'pain and toil' (Psalm 89.10), and my entire life will be full of you. You lift up the person whom you fill. But for the present, because I am not full of you, I am a burden to myself [...] There is a struggle between my regrets at my evil past and my memories of good joys, and which side has the victory I do not know. Alas, 'Lord have mercy upon me' (Psalm 30.10), wretch that I am. See, I do not hide my wounds. You are the physician, I am the patient [...]

It cannot be the case, almighty God, that your hand is not strong enough to cure all the sicknesses of my soul and, by a more abundant outflow of your grace, to extinguish the lascivious impulses of my sleep. You will more and more increase your gifts in me, Lord [...]

You give us many things when we pray, and whatever good we

received before we prayed for it, we have received from you. We have also received from you the grace that later we came to realize this [. . .]

See my condition! Weep with me and weep for me, you who have within yourselves a concern for the good, the springs from which good actions proceed [. . .] But you 'Lord my God, hear, look and see' (Psalm 12.4) and 'have mercy and heal me' (Psalm 79.15). In your eyes I have become a problem to myself, and that is my sickness [. . .]

In this immense jungle full of traps and dangers, see how many I have cut out and expelled from my heart, as you have granted me to do, 'God of my salvation' (Psalm 17.47; 37.23) [. . .]

But nothing can restore hope to us except your mercy, known since you began to transform us. You know how great a transformation you have brought about. You cured me in the first place of my lust for self-justification to show yourself propitious to all my other iniquities; you heal all my diseases, you redeem my life from corruptions, crown me with compassion and mercy, and satisfy my longing with good things (Psalm 102.3–5) [. . .]

I beseech you, my God, show me myself so that to my brothers who will pray for me I may confess what wound I am discovering in myself [. . .]

How you have loved us, good Father: you did not 'spare your only Son but delivered him up for us sinners' (Romans 8.32). How you have loved us, for whose sake 'he did not think it a usurpation to be equal to you and was made subject to the death of the cross' (Philippians 2.6, 8) [. . .] For us he was victorious before you and victor because he was victim [. . .] Before you he makes us sons instead of servants by being born of you and being servant to us. With good reason my firm hope is in him. For you will cure all my diseases (Psalm 102.3) through him who sits at your right hand and intercedes with you for us (Romans 8.34). Otherwise I would be in despair. Many and great are those diseases, many and great indeed. But your medicine is still more potent [. . .] 'Teach me and heal me' (Psalms 6.3; 142.10).

From *Confessions*, X. 38–9, 42, 45, 50, 56, 58, 62, 69–70, in H. Chadwick (tr.), *St Augustine: Confessions* (Oxford University Press, Oxford, 1991). (To look up Psalm references (10–148) in today's Bible, add one to the numbers given above.)

QUESTIONS TO PONDER

1. In his *Confessions* Augustine admits of a continuing struggle with passions and impulses and testifies of the liberation he has already received. How

can prayer be an experience of transformation and inner healing? Reflect upon your experiences of God as physician and healer.

2. Augustine was a great exponent of God's grace and speaks here of 'the abundant outflow of your grace'. How do you define grace? How do you experience grace in your prayer?

3. Augustine prays 'Show me myself'. What is the difference between God's gift of self-knowledge and introspection? How vital is this in seeking God's inner healing? Note why Augustine makes this request.

4. Augustine writes of 'expelling from the heart traps and dangers'. How can we empty ourselves of negative experiences through prayer?

5. Augustine places his hope in him who makes us 'sons not servants'. For Augustine the cross and resurrection change our status and give us new dignity. How would you express the changes in our identity and standing that Jesus Christ can bring us?

PRAYER EXERCISE

Either:

Try this exercise in seeking liberation in prayer using the expressiveness of hands. First, clench your fists and hold them before you. Let the tension you feel represent the stresses and worries you now face. Second, slowly open your hands, and as you release the tension believe that you are now 'letting go' and allowing your anxieties to fall into God's hands. Feel them draining from you. Third, turn your open palms upward and hold them out before you. This symbolizes your openness to God, your surrender to him and your need of his healing. Receptively, drink in the 'abundant outflow of God's grace'. If in a group, end by joining hands as a sign of solidarity and care for one another.

Or:

Noting how Augustine finds in the Psalms prayers with which he readily identifies, choose a Psalm from the Bible which you can make your own. Perhaps you could compose your own 'psalm' expressing your needs, hopes and thanksgivings.

FOR FURTHER READING

Burnaby, J., *Amor Dei*. Hodder & Stoughton, London, 1938; Canterbury Press, Norwich, 1991.

Towards a Christian Society: the Growth of Christendom

The 6th Century:
Benedict

THE SIXTH CENTURY became an age of turmoil and deep insecurity, the Roman empire continuing to disintegrate at the hands of successive barbarian invasions from the north, while from the east came troops despatched by the Byzantine emperor Justinian. He attempted to restore the political and religious unity of the empire, and managed to win back Italy from the Goths and to release north Africa from the stranglehold of the Vandals. But they were short-term successes, and Italy was once more in the control of barbarian forces.

It was in an Italy devastated by famine and attack that Gregory the Great began his papacy in the last decade of the century. He was the man for the moment, bringing courageous leadership and pastoral wisdom to a needy church and city, energetically organizing relief, providing new administration, and promoting missions for the conversion of barbarians. He represents the struggle of the Church to witness to charity and order in an age of conflict.

The year 597, which saw Gregory's apostle Augustine arrive at Canterbury to evangelize southern Britain, also witnessed the death of Columba on Iona. His monastery there was his base for a powerful ministry of evangelism throughout western Scotland. Both Columba and Augustine advanced their mission by achieving the conversion of local kings – Bridei, King of the Picts in Scotland, and Ethelbert in Kent. Though their spiritual heritage differed, both evangelists worked from a monastic foundation, Augustine arriving with some forty monks to begin his work. They represent complementary traditions in early British Christianity, Augustine the Catholic apostle sent from Rome, Columba reminding us of the crucial role of Celtic missionaries in the evangelization of significant parts of Britain.

BENEDICT (480–547) left Rome where he was educated at the start of the century, distressed by the city's disturbances and decadence. At the age of twenty, searching for solitude and a deeper encounter with God, he settled at

Subiaco, some thirty miles from Rome. A community began to form around him, and he went on to establish a colony of twelve new monasteries in the region. In 525 he moved to Monte Cassino where he composed his Rule for the guidance of monks.

Calling for openness to God in all things, the Rule opens with the words, 'Listen, my son, to the precepts of the master, and incline the ear of your heart; welcome the admonition of a loving father and put it into practice.' Benedict's aim was to provide a structure and framework for a life of seeking God. The monastery was to be a 'school in the Lord's service', a spiritual family living under the guidance of the abbot, their father in God. The vow of stability required monks to stay in one place for life, providing a rootedness in a turbulent world, while the vow of continual conversion required the monk to stay always open to the changes and challenges a life of prayer may bring. *Lectio divina*, 'sacred reading' or a reflective pondering of the texts of the Bible or the Fathers, was to lead into *meditatio*, meditation and prayer, always integrated into a life of work and worship.

A Reading from Benedict

As the Prophet says: Seven times a day have I spoken your praise (Psalm 119.164). We will fulfil this sacred number of seven if at Lauds, Prime, Terce, Sext, None, Vespers and Compline we render the obligations of our office [. . .]

The oratory is to be what it is called, and nothing else should be done or kept there. When the Work of God is finished all should go out in complete silence and with reverence for God, so that a brother who wishes to pray by himself will not be impeded by another's insensitivity. But if he wishes to pray in solitude, he should enter to pray with simplicity, not in a loud voice but with tears and attentiveness of heart. And therefore one who is not performing this work is not permitted to remain in the oratory after the Work of God, so that, as we said, no one else is impeded [. . .]

Idleness is the enemy of the soul; and therefore the brothers should be occupied at certain times in manual labour, and at certain other hours in sacred reading.

We therefore believe that the times for each may be ordered thus: from Easter to the first of October, on coming out of Prime they are to labour at whatever is necessary from the first until about the fourth hour; from the fourth hour until about the time they say Sext they are to devote themselves to reading; after Sext upon arising from table they are to rest on their beds in complete silence, or if anyone wishes to read to himself he may read, but without disturbing the others; and None is to be performed rather early at the middle of the eighth hour; then they are again to work at whatever needs to be done until Vespers.

If, however, local necessity or poverty require that they themselves are occupied with gathering the harvest, they should not be saddened; for they are then truly monks when they live by the labour of their hands, as did our fathers and the apostles. But everything is to be done with proper measure on account of the fainthearted [. . .]

The monastery cellarer [. . .] is to care for the sick, for children, for guests, and for the poor with all solicitude, knowing without doubt that for all these he will have to give an account on the Day of Judgement (cf. Luke 16.2). He is to look upon all the vessels and goods of the monastery as though they were the sacred vessels of the altar [. . .]

All guests who present themselves are to be received as Christ, for He will say: I was a stranger and you took me in (Matthew 25.35). And to everyone fitting honour is to be shown, especially to those of the household of faith (Galatians 6.10) and to pilgrims.

From *The Rule*, chapters 16, 52, 48, 31, 53, in L. Dysinger OSB (tr.), *The Rule of St Benedict in Latin and English* (Source Books, Trabuco Canyon, CA, 1994). For a British edition see Justin McCann (tr.), *The Rule of St Benedict* (Sheed & Ward, 1976). The 'Hours of Prayer' in the first paragraph correspond to Morning Prayer, first, third, sixth, ninth hours, Evening Prayer and Night Prayer.

QUESTIONS TO PONDER

1. The Rule of St Benedict aims to enable a structured life, where there is time and space for all tasks to be done, within a rhythm or pulse of prayer. What different aspects are allowed for in paragraph four? Do we maintain such a balance and perspective in our lives, juggling the demands of work, recreation and home?

2. Benedict directs that the Oratory should be respected as a space for prayer, never cluttered with items for storage. What steps can we take to safeguard such a space, physically or inwardly, which will not be overrun or eroded?

3. Why do you think Benedict calls the services in church 'the Work of God'? What does he mean by 'attentiveness of heart'?

4. Key words in the Rule are 'respect' and 'reverence' – for all things and for all tasks. The cellarer is to handle all things as sacred vessels and humdrum

jobs are as important as 'noble' ones. How can we train ourselves to live with such a sacramental view of life today? What ideas do you have for seeing God in all things?

5. Although his Rule encourages a keen sense of order in life, Benedict allows compassionately for human weakness and for unexpected events. Guests are to be welcomed as Christ, not resented as intrusions. What sort of happenings or people 'interrupt' our day? How can we deal with them positively?

PRAYER EXERCISE

Either:

On a clean piece of paper draw a circle to represent your life. Divide it up into different sized segments representing the proportions of time you normally spend on tasks and commitments. Reflect on whether there is a right balance between work and play, prayer and activity (this can be done in pairs in a group). Notice the tension between possible fragmentedness and the whole-ness of the circle. Conclude by placing the papers under a cross as a sign of surrendering our often frantic lives to the Lordship of Christ.

Or:

Make a review of the last twenty-four hours. Reflect on how you used your time. Where was God in all this? How did you handle interruptions or unexpected challenges? Did you find yourself resenting any task? Were you able to meet strangers in a spirit where they were 'received as Christ'? Be penitent for negative attitudes or opportunities missed. Praise God for the times you were aware of his presence. Conclude with Psalm 139.

FOR FURTHER READING

Taylor, B. C., *Spirituality for Everyday Living: An Adaptation of the Rule of St Benedict*. Liturgical Press, Minnesota, 1989.
de Waal, E., *Seeking God*. Fount, London, 1984.

The 7th Century:
Maximus the Confessor

THE SEVENTH CENTURY was a testing time for the Christian Church – a time of fresh challenges and exciting opportunities.

In Britain the Roman missionaries continued their advance from the south, while in the north Aidan, a monk of Iona, evangelized from his base at Lindisfarne. The two traditions, Celtic and Roman, came face to face at the Synod of Whitby in 664, which endorsed Roman influence in worship and teaching in Britain.

Bursting into the Middle East and Mediterranean lands the new religion of Islam advanced with a zeal and ferocity that took all by surprise. Dedicated to the concept of holy war (jihad), the Arab conquerors swept across Christianized lands with a ruthless determination – Jerusalem was captured in 638, Alexandria and Antioch followed, and Cyprian's and Augustine's congregations in North Africa were decimated. With the decline of such ancient Christian centres, the role of the patriarchate of Constantinople grew stronger, leading the Eastern Church in a shrinking Byzantine empire, while its relationship with Rome steadily waned.

MAXIMUS the Confessor (580–662) has been called the 'Father of Byzantine theology' because his ideas and terminology were to shape expressions of Eastern spirituality for centuries. He fused into a brilliant synthesis rich ideas from the early Church Fathers and later thinking about the mystery of union with God. He taught that the purpose of history was the incarnation of God's Son to enable the divinization of humankind, restoring God's image in us distorted by Adam's sin. In his analysis of the human search for God, Maximus identified three elements in our spiritual makeup or soul – the intellect, the passionate part and the desiring part. He believed that our passions can be transformed into a perfect love for God.

Born into an aristocratic family, Maximus had been chief secretary to the Emperor Heraclius. In 614 he renounced this career, and became a monk near

Constantinople; later he was elected abbot. He moved to north Africa to escape Persian invasions, and then lived in Rome, helping Pope Martin in his stand for orthodox teaching about the person of Christ. This stand led to his downfall. A gifted and articulate teacher, he came into conflict with the heretical Emperor Constans II, who had his tongue torn out. He died in exile soon afterwards in 662. But his influence lived on and his *Four Centuries on Love* has been described as 'one of the most profound and beautiful works in all Christian writing'.

A Reading from Maximus the Confessor

He who truly loves God prays entirely without distraction, and he who prays entirely without distraction loves God truly. But he whose intellect is fixed on any worldly thing does not pray without distraction, and consequently he does not love God.

The intellect that dallies with some sensible thing clearly is attached to it by some passion, such as desire, irritation, anger or rancour; and unless it becomes detached from that thing it will not be able to free itself from the passion affecting it.

When passions dominate the intellect, they separate it from God, binding it to material things and preoccupying it with them. But when love of God dominates the intellect, it frees it from its bonds, persuading it to rise above not only sensible things but even this transitory life [. . .]

Unless various successive spiritual contemplations also occupy the intellect, the practice of virtues by itself cannot free it so entirely from passions that it is able to pray undistractedly. Practice of the virtues frees the intellect only from dissipation and hatred; spiritual contemplation releases it also from forgetfulness and ignorance. In this way the intellect can pray as it should [. . .]

The reward of self-control is dispassion, and the reward of faith is spiritual knowledge. Dispassion engenders discrimination, and spiritual knowledge engenders love for God.

When the intellect practises the virtues correctly, it advances in moral understanding. When it practises contemplation, it advances in spiritual knowledge. The first leads the spiritual contestant to discriminate between virtue and vice; the second leads the participant to the inner qualities of incorporeal and corporeal things. Finally, the intellect is granted the grace of theology when, carried on wings of love beyond these two former stages, it is taken up into God and with the help of the

Holy Spirit discerns – as far as this is possible for the human intellect – the qualities of God [...]

[T]ry to discern, as far as possible, the qualities that appertain to His nature – qualities of eternity, infinity, indeterminateness, goodness, wisdom, and the power of creating, preserving and judging creatures, and so on. For he who discovers these qualities, to however small an extent, is a great theologian.

He who combines the practice of the virtues with spiritual knowledge is a man of power. For with the first he withers his desire and tames his incensiveness, and with the second he gives wings to his intellect and goes out of himself to God [...]

When a man's intellect is constantly with God, his desire grows beyond all measure into an intense longing for God and his incensiveness is completely transformed into divine love. For by continual participation in the divine radiance his intellect becomes totally filled with light; and when it has reintegrated its passible aspect, it redirects this aspect towards God, as we have said, filling it with an incomprehensible and intense longing for Him and with unceasing love, thus drawing it entirely away from worldly things to the divine [...]

The intellect joined to God for long periods through prayer and love becomes wise, good, powerful, compassionate, merciful and long-suffering; in short, it includes within itself almost all the divine qualities. But when the intellect withdraws from God and attaches itself to material things, either it becomes self-indulgent like some domestic animal, or like a wild beast it fights with men for the sake of these things [...]

The principal vices – stupidity, cowardice, licentiousness, injustice – are the 'image' of the 'earthy' man. The principal virtues – intelligence, courage, self-restraint, justice – are the 'image' of the 'heavenly' man. As we have borne the image of the earthy, let us also bear the image of the heavenly (cf. 1 Corinthians 15.49).

From *Four Hundred Texts on Love*, Second Century 1–3, 5, 25–8, 48, 52, 79, in G. E. H. Palmer, P. Sherrard and K. Ware (trs and eds), *The Philokalia Vol. 2* (Faber & Faber, London, 1981).

QUESTIONS TO PONDER

1. Maximus depicts prayer as a struggle – in the intellect or will of man – between selfish earth-bound passions and a desire for God. Is this true to your experience?

The Spirit is willing but the flesh weak
Sometimes what seems a desire for god is really
disguised earth-bound passions

2. 'By continual participation in the divine radiance his intellect becomes totally filled with light [. . .] it redirects [its passions] towards God.' Maximus believed that through prayer we can decisively redirect our fiery energies and desires ('incensiveness') into love for God. How would you describe the changes God can work in us in prayer – reshaping our drives and outlook?

3. For Maximus the goal is discovering the qualities of God, through gaining spiritual knowledge. To what extent do you think we can actually 'know' God? In what ways could God be 'unknowable'?

4. 'He who combines the practice of the virtues with spiritual knowledge is a man of power.' For Maximus, we should become more like God himself by 'the practice of the virtues'. In what ways can prayer enable us to live a more holy life? How can 'knowing God' change the way we live? Read Galatians 5.22–5 for clues.

5. What else strikes you about Maximus' teaching? At which points do you agree and disagree with him?

PRAYER EXERCISE

Either:

Try to express your view of our human calling and destiny. For Maximus, we must allow God, working in partnership with our will and decisiveness, to redirect our self-indulgent passions towards him, so that we progressively become more like him, ourselves embracing the divine qualities – this is the Orthodox concept of human deification through Christ. What is your vision? Noting Maximus' encouraging words 'He who discovers [God's] qualities [. . .] is a great theologian', write out key words that you would use to describe the goal and route of discipleship – or express your vision pictorially or symbolically on a piece of paper.

Or:

Noting how Maximus identifies the passions as the 'battleground' of prayer, read Paul's account in Romans 7.15–8.11. Give thanks for the work of the Holy Spirit in your life, enabling victory and Christlikeness.

FOR FURTHER READING

Lossky, V., *The Mystical Theology of the Eastern Church*. James Clarke, Cambridge, 1973.

Meyendorf, J., *Byzantine Theology*. Mowbrays, London, 1974.

The 8th Century:
St Patrick's Breastplate

THE EIGHTH CENTURY saw some advances in evangelism. Since the late sixth century monks from the Irish-Celtic church had led missions into Europe, courageously sharing the faith but attending little to the task of consolidation. Now, Anglo-Saxon evangelists continued this work, underpinned by a stronger Roman sense of church organization. Boniface from Crediton was consecrated bishop for the German people and laboured for the gospel in Bavaria and beyond. He played a key part in the revival of the Church in Gaul, working under King Pepin to bring a measure of organizational reform and intellectual renewal.

This development in learning developed further under Pepin's son Charlemagne. As a military leader, Charles the Great aimed to be a sort of second Constantine for the West, securing by successive triumphs political unity for a fragmented Europe. As an educationalist, he pioneered new forms of training for the clergy, aided by the energetic scholar Alcuin, establishing schools at hundreds of monasteries and cathedrals. This achievement, kindling a remarkable recovery of interest in classical and early Christian literature by the industrious copying of ancient manuscripts, was later to be called the 'Carolingian Renaissance'. But the developments in worship Charlemagne inspired were not so constructive. During these years the eucharist ceased to be the community at prayer. Mass was offered in the Latin tongue by a priest at a distant altar, his back to the people. Charlemagne sought to standardize liturgical practice throughout his empire, insisting on forms of worship which, while impressive and ceremonious, had become remote from ordinary people.

In the East, bitter arguments over worship had erupted earlier when Byzantine Emperor Leo III publicly smashed a revered icon of Christ in Constantinople. He had come to see icons as an idolatrous barrier to the conversion of Muslims and Jews and in 726 ordered all to be destroyed. It was the monks who were in the front line of their defence, many dying in rioting and bitter conflict. They upheld their conviction that icons had a proper part to play in both worship and teaching.

Far away, at the very edges of Europe – and even beyond the reaches of the former Roman empire – Celtic spirituality had been developing its own distinctive character. Centred on monastic foundations, it saw a new flowering in the eighth century, expressing itself in beautiful religious poetry. At this time there was a new interest in the figure of St Patrick who had played such a key role in evangelization three hundred years earlier. Prayers became attributed to him because they sought to represent and develop the rich tradition he helped to establish.

St Patrick's Breastplate

I rise today
    in power's strength, invoking the Trinity,
    believing in threeness,
    confessing the oneness,
    of creation's Creator.

I rise today
    in the power of Christ's birth and baptism,
    in the power of his crucifixion and burial,
    in the power of his rising and ascending,
    in the power of his descending and judging.

I rise today
    in the power of the love of cherubim,
    in the obedience of angels,
    and service of archangels,
    in hope of rising to receive the reward,
    in the prayers of patriarchs,
    in the predictions of prophets,
    in the preaching of apostles,
    in the faith of confessors,
    in the innocence of holy virgins,
    in the deeds of the righteous [. . .]

I rise today
    with the power of God to pilot me,
    God's strength to sustain me,
    God's wisdom to guide me,
    God's eye to look ahead for me,
    God's ear to hear me,

God's word to speak for me,
God's hand to protect me,
God's way before me,
God's shield to defend me,
God's host to deliver me:
  from snares of devils,
  from evil temptations,
  from nature's failings,
  from all who wish to harm me,
  far or near,
  alone and in a crowd.

Around me I gather today all these powers
  against every cruel and merciless force
  to attack my body and soul,
  against the charms of false prophets,
  the black laws of paganism,
  the false laws of heretics,
  the deceptions of idolatry [. . .]

May Christ protect me today
  against poison and burning,
  against drowning and wounding,
  so that I may have abundant reward;
  Christ with me, Christ before me, Christ behind me;
  Christ within me, Christ beneath me, Christ above me;
  Christ to right of me, Christ to left of me;
  Christ in my lying, Christ in my sitting, Christ in my rising;
  Christ in the heart of all who think of me,
  Christ in the tongue of all who speak to me,
  Christ in the eye of all who see me,
  Christ in the ear of all who hear me.

I rise today
  in power's strength, invoking the Trinity,
  believing in threeness,
  confessing the oneness,
  of creation's Creator.

For to the Lord belongs salvation,
and to the Lord belongs salvation
and to Christ belongs salvation.

May your salvation, Lord, be with us always.

From 'St Patrick's Breastplate',
in O. Davies and F. Bowie, *Celtic Christian Spirituality* (SPCK,
London, and the Continuum Publishing Group, New York, 1995).

QUESTIONS TO PONDER

1. 'I rise today [. . .] invoking the Trinity.' This Celtic 'breastplate' prayer seeks God's protection at the start of a new day. How do you begin each day? How do you view each day – as God's gift, as a fresh chance to discover God? Noting a possible link with baptism in the first verse, how can we renew our sense of being consecrated and dedicated to Christ each morning?

2. 'I rise today in the power of Christ's birth and baptism.' Christ's life is ours – bound up and throbbing in our life. How can we relate and connect with the events of Christ's life which are, in a sense, distant in time? Looking in turn at each of the eight Christ-events mentioned in this verse, describe what power or influence they might have in your tasks and responsibilities today.

3. 'I rise today [. . .] in the prayers of patriarchs.' The Apostles' Creed says 'I believe in the communion of saints' – a solidarity and union with the saints – and here verse three speaks of a personal relationship to the angels and saints, placing the individual 'I' of the prayer in the context of a community which transcends heaven and earth. What is your experience of the saints and the angels? Are there times when you feel conscious of the strength and inspiration of other Christians, whether living or departed?

4. 'I gather all these powers against every cruel and merciless force.' What does this poem reveal about the dangers faced by the Celtic Christians? What dangers, spiritual or material, threaten our discipleship today? How important to you is the idea of spiritual warfare? Reflect on the protection God offers us in Ephesians 6.10–20.

5. 'May your salvation, Lord, be with us always.' What is your understanding of salvation – from what, for what? How should it affect our daily tasks and outlook?

PRAYER EXERCISE

Either:

Express the sixth verse as an 'action prayer' or 'enacted prayer' using your hands and body expressively while it is very slowly spoken.

Or:
Reflecting on verse six, identify the different ways Christ is present in the world today. Look up these presences of Christ in the Bible: Matthew 25.35–40; Luke 22.19; John 1.3; 1 Corinthians 12.27.

FOR FURTHER READING

Adam, D., *The Cry of the Deer: Meditations on the Hymn of St Patrick*. Triangle, London, 1987.

The 9th Century:
Oengus the Culdee

THE NINTH CENTURY opened with a symbolic, political and religious act that was to have far-reaching repercussions, when in St Peter's Rome on Christmas Day 800 Charlemagne was crowned Emperor of the West by Pope Leo III. His hope – unfulfilled – was to limit the Church to spiritual matters, but a struggle persisted: pope and emperor were now the two centres of power in Western society. Charlemagne's coronation, representing a proud rejection of the claims of Constantinople, further fractured the already fragile relationship between the West and the Byzantine empire.

The ninth century was a time of new evangelization. Cyril and Methodius were sent by the Patriarch of Constantinople to bring the Good News to the Slav peoples. They invented a Slavonic alphabet in order to translate the Gospels and to provide a language for worship. Its use in mission was to spread to the people of Bulgaria and Russia.

In the East, the painful dispute over the use of icons concluded with victory for their supporters. Now a rich and hard-won theology underpinned their devotional use. The sacred use of material elements was understood to be a continual reminder of the God who took on flesh in the incarnation. The icons were to represent the return of God's creation to him in worship, the first-fruits of the new creation and 'windows of heaven'. Meanwhile, in quite a different context, it was delight in God's creation that continued to characterize the spirituality of the Celtic tradition.

✠

OENGUS the Culdee (c. 765–839) was born into one of the Irish royal families. After an education at one of the monastic schools, he resolved to seek God in solitude amidst the unspoilt scenery of rural Ireland on the banks of the River Nore. Later he joined a group of monks near Dublin, becoming both abbot and bishop.

Traditionally a 'Culdee', Oengus is associated with a revival of radical monasticism in the eighth century known as the 'Companions (or Friends) of

God', which aimed to recover the ancient forms of asceticism, and which spread to the west coast of Britain. It was to preserve for some centuries the Celtic tradition in Ireland in the face of the gradual domination of Catholicism.

The movement produced works of art and the most beautiful religious poetry, exemplified here in the *Celtic Psalter* attributed to Oengus, a retelling of the story of the Bible in 150 short poems, like the Psalms of David. Celebrating the goodness of the heart of creation, it testifies to the Celtic joy in finding God in earth, sky and sea. But it also reflects the Celtic experience of the closeness of the heavenly world, its author believed in tradition to have often conversed with angels!

A Reading from Oengus the Culdee

Creation of the world

My dear King, my own King, without pride, without sin, you created the whole world, eternal, victorious King.

King above the elements, King above the sun, King beneath the ocean, King of the north and south, the east and west, against you no enemy can prevail.

King of the Mysteries, you existed before the elements, before the sun was set in the sky, before the waters covered the ocean floor; beautiful King, you are without beginning and without end.

King, you created the daylight, and made the darkness; you are not arrogant or boastful, and yet strong and firm.

King, you created the land out of shapeless mass, you carved the mountains and chiselled the valleys, and covered the earth with trees and grass.

King, you stretched out the sky above the earth, a perfect sphere like a perfect apple, and you decorated the sky with stars to shine at night.

King, you pierced the earth with springs from which pure water flows, to form streams and rivers across the land [. . .]

King, you measured each object and each span within the universe: the heights of the mountains and the depths of the oceans; the distance from the sun to the moon, and from star to star.

You ordained the movements of every object: the sun to cross the sky each day, and the moon to rise each night; the clouds to carry rain from the sea, and the rivers to carry water back to the sea [. . .]

And you created men and women to be your stewards of the earth, always praising you for your boundless love.

Creation of heaven

King, you created heaven according to your delight, a place that is safe and pure, its air filled with the songs of angels.

It is like a strong mighty city, which no enemy can invade, with walls as high as mountains.

It is like an open meadow, in which all can move freely, with people arriving from earth but never leaving.

It is huge, ten times the size of earth, so that every creature ever born can find a place.

It is small, no bigger than a village, where all are friends, and none is a stranger [. . .]

Round the lawn walks a King, not dressed in fine robes, but in a simple white tunic, smiling, and embracing those he meets [. . .]

From *The Celtic Psalter*,
in R. Van de Weyer, *Celtic Fire: An Anthology of Celtic Christian Literature*
(Darton, Longman & Todd, London, and Doubleday, New York, 1990).

Questions to Ponder

1. Oengus, himself from a local royal family, experienced the person of 'King' to be someone who lives close to his people, among his kith and kin. Note here how his majestic God is found in the very midst of creation. Recall from the Gospels how Jesus taught about the reign or Kingdom of God through parables of nature. Start with Matthew chapter 13. What kind of King does Jesus envisage God to be? How does this compare with Oengus' ideas?

2. Someone once wrote, 'Your God is too small.' How does Oengus challenge us to recapture a cosmic, yet tender, view of God?

3. 'And you created men and women to be your stewards of the earth.' What role should ecological awareness play in today's spirituality? What positive

steps should our prayers lead us to take – in ordering our own lifestyle, and in getting involved in local and global issues?

4. Read again Oengus' description of heaven. What is your vision? What imagery would you use to depict your hopes? Compare John's picture in Revelation 21.10–22.5.

5. What poems, pictures or icons have inspired you in your spiritual journey?

PRAYER EXERCISE

Either:

Working with the Creator Spirit, make something creative to express love for God your King: paint a picture, make a collage or sculpture, compose a poem or song, listen to a piece of music that can lead you into prayer. Whatever you choose, do it in a spirit of worship, offering it to God in thanksgiving.

Or:

Take time to get back in touch with nature in a prayerful way. Go on a 'prayer-walk' in your locality, asking God to awaken each of your five senses. Look carefully at the details of leaves; feel the textures of different objects; listen out for all sorts of sounds; smell fragrances – and find something nice to taste!

FOR FURTHER READING

McLean, G., *Praying with Celtic Christians*. Triangle, London, 1996.

Newell, P., *Listening for the Heartbeat of God: A Celtic Spirituality*. SPCK, London, 1997.

The 10th Century:
Simeon the New Theologian

THE TENTH CENTURY was, for the West, later to be characterized 'the Dark Ages'. A time of deep instability and uncertainty ensued. The office of Emperor dissolved at the start of the century, the Carolingian empire fragmented and civil order steadily broke down. Europe was attacked on all sides – by Viking Norsemen from Scandinavia, by Magyar warriors from the east, by Muslim Saracens from the south. As a new millennium came on the horizon, many feared the end of the world. Only developing feudalism, with its threefold structure of overlord, vassal and serf gave some semblance of order to society, and the Church, as landowner, became entangled in this unjust system. While churches were plundered by invaders, powerful feudal lords manipulated church appointments to their own ends. The spiritual life of the Church in the West was at a very low ebb.

However, there were signs of hope. The French Abbey of Cluny was founded in 910, destined to become a wellspring of renewal in the next century. In 962 the empire was revived as a Romano-Germanic alliance when the Pope crowned Otto the Great as King. Evangelization advanced into Poland and among the Hungarian peoples.

The conversion of Russia to Orthodoxy is recorded in the *Russian Chronicles*. They tell the story of how Vladimir, Prince of Kiev, sent envoys far and wide to research the religious landscape. Vladimir was not impressed by their accounts of Islam, Judaism and Latin Christianity. However, they related to him that when they entered the Church of Holy Wisdom in Constantinople, such was the beauty of worship they did not know whether they were in earth or heaven. So Vladimir made his choice, and his own baptism in 989 was followed by mass baptism of the Russian people.

Certainly, this was a time of achievement of Orthodoxy, while the Byzantine empire enjoyed a period of cultural prosperity. Not yet separate from Western Catholicism but with its own increasingly distinctive worship and outlook, it had at its heart the deep rivers of monastic life. Monasticism took a big step forward when the first *lavra* (colony of monks) was established on the Greek peninsula of Athos. This was to become 'the holy

Women are
not allowed

mountain', growing into a republic of monks and the centre of Orthodox spirituality.

✠

SIMEON (949–1022) was based at Constantinople where, for twenty-five years, he was abbot of St Mamas monastery. He has been called in the East 'the greatest mystic of the Middle Ages', and was surnamed 'the New Theologian' by later admirers to identify him with such creative theologians as St John. He anticipated the later Byzantine tradition of prayer known as hesychasm (from a Greek word meaning 'quietness' or 'stillness') with his teaching on personal communion with God in contemplation. His central conviction was that the Holy Spirit makes possible a conscious encounter with Christ and, in some sense, the vision of God in this life. In an age when doctrinal controversy over the work of the Spirit divided the Greek and Latin churches – because of the Western addition to the Nicene Creed, 'We believe in the Holy Spirit, who proceeds from the Father *and the Son*' – Simeon taught the importance of personal experience of the Spirit, within the eucharistic community of the Church.

A Reading from Simeon the New Theologian

But answer this question: What is the Holy Spirit? 'God,' you say, 'we confess Him as true God from true God.' Thus, as you see and in accordance with the dogmas of the Church, you say that He is God. So, too, by both saying and thinking that He is true God proceeding from true God, you establish that those who have the Holy Spirit have confessedly God dwelling always within themselves [. . .]

Make no mistake! God is a fire, and has come as fire, and has cast fire on the earth. The same Fire goes about looking for kindling to seize upon, for a ready disposition and will, in order to fall upon it and ignite it [. . .] Afterwards, when it has completely cleansed us of the filth of the passions, it becomes food and drink, light and joy without ceasing in us, and by participation, it makes us light ourselves. It is like a clay pot that has been set on the fire. At first it is somewhat blackened by the smoke of the burning fuel, but after the fuel has begun to burn fiercely, then it becomes all translucent and like the fire itself, and the smoke can communicate none of its blackness to it. Just so, indeed, does the soul which has begun to burn with divine longing see first of all the murk of

the passions within it, billowing out like smoke in the fire of the Holy
Spirit [...] After these things have been utterly destroyed [...] then the
divine and immaterial fire unites itself essentially to the soul, too, and the
latter is immediately kindled and becomes transparent, and shares in it
like the clay pot does in the visible fire [...]

What else is so dear to God and welcome as a contrite and humble
heart, and pride laid low in a spirit of humility? It is in such a
condition of soul that God Himself comes to dwell and make His rest,
and that every machination of the devil remains ineffective. All the
corrupting passions of sin vanish completely. The fruit of the Holy
Spirit alone weighs heavy in the soul, that fruit which is love, joy,
peace, kindness, goodness, faith, meekness, humility, all-embracing
continence, followed in succession and beauty by divine knowledge,
the wisdom of the Word, and the abyss of Christ's hidden counsels
and mysteries. He who has arrived at becoming and being endowed
with these qualities is changed for the good, and from a man he
becomes an angel. In the body here-below he circulates among men,
but in his spirit he lives and converses with the angels, and in joy
inexpressible stretches himself out to the love of God. To that love
no one among men has ever drawn near unless first he purified his
heart through repentance and many tears, and penetrated the depths
of humility, and became pregnant with the Holy Spirit, by the grace
and love for mankind of our Lord Jesus Christ, with Whom be glory,
honour, and majesty to the Father together with the Holy Spirit, now
and ever, and unto ages of ages. Amen.

'Have mercy on me, Son of David, and open the eyes of my soul, so that I
may see the light of the world, even You, Who are God, and may become
even I, a son of the day [...] O Merciful One, send the Comforter even to
me, so that He may teach me the things concerning You; and, O God of
all, declare what is Yours to me. Illumine me with the true light, O
Compassionate One, so that I may see the glory which You had with
Your Father before the world was made. Abide even in me, as You have
said, so that I, too, may become worthy of abiding in You, and may then
consciously enter into You and consciously possess You within myself
[...]'

From *Ethical Discourses* 5, 7, 8,
in A. Golitzin (tr.), *St Symeon the New Theologian: On the Mystical Life:
The Ethical Discourses* (St Vladimir's Seminary Press, New York, 1996).

QUESTIONS TO PONDER

1. 'Those who have the Holy Spirit have God dwelling always within themselves.' Simeon's concern is that we enter into the full reality of the doctrine that the Spirit of God actually dwells within us. How can we become more conscious and aware of the presence of the Holy Spirit in our lives?
2. Simeon insists that brokenness and penitence are prerequisites for receiving the Spirit. What are the things which stop us from experiencing the Spirit more fully, forming barriers to him?
3. In his prayer, the New Theologian describes the Spirit in language from St John. How would you describe the role of the Holy Spirit in prayer? Compare John 14.25f; 16.7f; Romans 8.14f, 26f.
4. 'Open the eyes of my soul, so that I may see the light of the world, even You, Who are God.' In what ways can we experience the vision of God in this life?
5. What do you think Simeon means by 'becoming pregnant with the Holy Spirit'? *You can't get pregnant if your tubes are blocked.*

PRAYER EXERCISE

Either:
Reflect on the idea 'God is a fire'. First, on pieces of paper write sins or barriers to the Spirit and burn these in a small brazier or tin: the cleansing fire of the Spirit. Then, as the fire burns, add incense grains to express the light and joy of the Spirit who enables prayer, reading aloud Simeon's second paragraph.

Or:
'Illumine me with the true light.' In the darkness, light a candle, perhaps the Easter candle, as a prayer focus. Compose a litany to the Holy Spirit, using different titles for him: 'Spirit of ..., Come to us!' End by slowly reading Simeon's prayer.

FOR FURTHER READING

Meyendorf, J., *Byzantine Theology*. Mowbrays, London, 1974.

Medieval Spiritualities:
the High Middle Ages

The 11th Century:
Anselm

/(cnu - West   *East Constantinople*

THE ELEVENTH CENTURY saw the fault lines between the Church in the West and the Byzantine Church widen into an unbridgeable gap. The division was formalized with the mutual exchange of anathemas between pope and patriarch in 1054. Political rivalry between the two empires of Rome and Constantinople had been compounded by a failure of understanding between Latin West and Greek East and seemingly irreconcilable liturgical and theological differences.

The Crusades were to worsen relationships further. These almost annual campaigns for the West began in 1095, with the double object of defeating Muslim 'infidels' and securing access to the holy places – Jerusalem was held in 1099. But this was an exploitation of religious objectives to justify often violent military purposes.

In England, William's conquest in 1066 – with papal blessing – marked the passing of the Anglo-Saxon period into Norman times. He worked with Lanfranc, Archbiship of Canterbury, to implement some of the reforms sought by Pope Gregory VII, who was trying to revitalize the Western Church by setting in motion a series of radical measures. The sale of clerical posts for profit (simony) was brought to an end in England, and first steps were made to enforce priestly celibacy.

ANSELM (1033–1109) became Lanfranc's successor at Canterbury towards the end of the century. He had entered the great Abbey of Bec in Normandy in 1059, after a turbulent youth. There he learnt much from Lanfranc who was abbot at the time, and emerged as a wise spiritual director and great thinker, becoming prior at the age of thirty. He described his religious quest as 'faith seeking understanding' and is called 'the Father of Scholasticism', writing many influential books which combined a robust rational defence of belief with a tenderness of devotion.

When he became Archbishop of Canterbury he had much less time for such writing, because of painful struggles with the Conqueror's unbelieving son, who wanted the Crown to interfere with the running of the Church. It was when he was exiled to Rome that Anselm wrote what has been called 'the most significant treatise on the Incarnation to come out of the Middle Ages' – a work called 'Why did God become man?' – concluding that Jesus came for the supreme purpose of bringing us peace with God through the cross.

In addition to these great works of theology, Anselm composed many prayers which he shared with the intention that they be used as 'raw material' for reflection and prayer. In a Preface to his collection he wrote, 'The purpose of the prayers and meditations that follow is to stir up the mind of the reader to the love or fear of God, or to self-examination. They are not to be read in a turmoil, but quietly, not skimmed or hurried through, but taken a little at a time, with deep and thoughtful meditation.'

A Reading from Anselm of Canterbury

Heart of my soul, stir yourself up as much as ever you can [. . .]
and let all that is within me praise the good Mary has done,
    love the blessing she has received,
wonder at her loftiness, and beseech her kindness;
    for I need her defence daily,
and in my need I desire, implore, and beseech it [. . .]

For he was born of a mother to take our nature,
and to make us, by restoring our life, sons of his mother.
He invites us to confess ourselves his brethren.
    So our judge is our brother,
    the Saviour of the world is our brother,
and finally our God through Mary is our brother.
With what confidence then ought we to hope,
    and thus consoled how can we fear,
when our salvation or damnation hangs on the will
    of a good brother and a devoted mother? [. . .]
With what familiarity should we commit ourselves to them,
    with what security may we flee to them!
For our good brother forgives us when we sin,
    and turns away from us what our errors deserve,
    he gives us what in penitence we ask.

The good mother prays and beseeches for us,
  she asks and pleads that he may hear us favourably.
She pleads with the son on behalf of the sons,
  the only-begotten for the adopted,
  the lord for the servants [. . .]

Mary, how much we owe you, Mother and Lady,
  by whom we have such a brother!
What thanks and praise can we return to you?
Great Lord, our elder brother,
  great Lady, our best of mothers,
teach my heart a sweet reverence in thinking of you.
  You are good, and so are you;
  you are gentle, and so are you.
  Speak and give my soul the gift
of remembering you with love, delighting in you,
rejoicing in you, so that I may come to you.
  Let me rise up to your love.
Desiring to be always with you, my heart is sick of love,
  my soul melts in me, my flesh fails.
  If only my inmost being might be on fire
  with the sweet fervour of your love [. . .]
  If only the spirit within me
might come close to the sweetness of your love [. . .]

From *Prayer to St Mary (3)*,
in B. Ward (tr.), *Prayers and Meditations of St Anselm* (Penguin,
Harmondsworth, 1973).

QUESTIONS TO PONDER

1. Anselm looks to Mary and the saints as examples of openness to God, as
   models of holiness. He honours what God has done in Mary: 'Love the
   blessing she has received.' Reflecting on the story of the annunciation in
   Luke 1.26–38, what can you learn from the way Mary responded to God's
   call?

2. 'The good mother prays and beseeches.' Anselm goes further and finds in
   Mary a friend and intercessor in heaven, to whose prayers he commends
   himself unreservedly. He believes that in the Body of Christ there is no
   divide between heaven and earth, but all are united in a bond of mutual
   love and prayer. What is your view of the proper relationship we can have

with God's saints? How can a real friendship with them deepen our relationship with God and with his Church?

3. 'Our God through Mary is our brother.' Relationships are changed because of God's incarnation in Christ, and by faith and baptism we are incorporated as members of God's family. Making parallels with human family life, what are the implications of belonging to a spiritual family? Compare Matthew 12.46–50; John 19.25–7; Romans 8.29.

4. This intensely personal prayer of Anselm reveals the role of both real mental effort and honest desire in prayer: 'Heart of my soul, stir yourself up as much as ever you can'; 'Desiring to be always with you, my heart is sick of love'. For Anselm, prayer begins with a preparing of the mind for Godward thoughts, and includes a sense of longing and yearning for union with him. What part do these features play in your own praying?

5. Anselm composed prayers to many saints, including John, Peter, Stephen, Mary Magdalene and Benedict. What saints or characters from the Bible inspire you – and why? If you have a saint's name yourself, what inspiration can you draw from your name-saint?

PRAYER EXERCISE

Either:

Reflect on your own relationship with Mary by praying imaginatively the story of the visitation in Luke 1.39–56. Picture yourself in Elizabeth's place in this joyful encounter. What news have you to share, what joys and sorrows, with Mary?

Or:

Following Anselm's example, write a prayer-letter to a saint with whom you especially identify. What aspects of their example create a sense of solidarity with your own situation?

FOR FURTHER READING

Thornton, M., *English Spirituality*. SPCK, London, 1963.

The 12ᵗʰ Century:
Bernard of Clairvaux

THE TWELFTH CENTURY was the brightest period of medieval Christendom in the West with a strong papacy, monastic revival and a flowering of sacramental theology. Architecture reflected a new confidence and spiritual yearning. Round-arched Romanesque buildings competed with the emerging Gothic architecture which reached up to heaven with its soaring vaults and taught the gospel story through stained glass and sculpture. Majestic new cathedrals provided an awesome setting for beautiful worship. But this other-worldly architecture and mysterious liturgy were balanced by a new devotion to the humanity of Christ shown in passion plays and in fresh interest in pilgrimage to the Holy Land – engendered by the continuing Crusades.

In England, the Church faced renewed struggles with the monarchy. Henry II longed to curb its power, and claimed the right to appoint bishops himself. Archbishop Thomas à Becket stood up for the freedom of the Church from such interference and in 1170, after returning to Canterbury from six years of exile in France, he was murdered in his own cathedral. Hailed as a martyr and attributed miracles at his tomb, Thomas was canonized just three years later, and Canterbury became an important centre of pilgrimage for Christians from all over Europe.

In many places, the Church enjoyed spiritual renewal through the formation of new monastic orders. The Cistercians, based at Cîteaux, attracted many with their radical return to simplicity and solitude, a strict lifestyle of prayer and labour which embraced lay brothers.

BERNARD (1090–1153) was a young nobleman of twenty-one when he left his home to join the monastery at Cîteaux, together with thirty other young men from Burgundy. The steady increase of numbers necessitated the building of new monasteries, and within three years Bernard was asked by the abbot to find a location for a new foundation. He established a community at

Clairvaux, destined to become one of the most influential centres of monastic spirituality for generations.

Bernard went on to establish a further sixty-six abbeys. He was active in the wider Church as teacher, preacher and reformer and his influence stretched throughout Europe. Though earlier resolved to renounce the world, Bernard, a determined and principled man, allowed himself to become caught up with the issues of the day, intervening in the selection of a Cistercian pope, and even supporting the second Crusade with his preaching. But his greatest achievement was encouraging the spread of Cistercian spirituality, through personal involvement and by his writings.

They reveal a deep mystical spirit, a great grasp of the Scriptures and a warm Christ-centred devotion. A chief theme was the analysis of the relationship of the soul with God and Bernard wrote with profound and sensitive understanding. In *On the Love of God*, he urged a purifying of motives for devotion, arguing that we should love God not for what we can get out of it, but for his delight alone. Like others before him, Bernard found in the Song of Songs a source of rich imagery with which to describe the inner life of prayer.

A Reading from Bernard of Clairvaux

Previously the Bridegroom had been called 'the king', now he is called, 'my lover'. Before he was in his royal banqueting room, now he is happy to be with his bride. Humility is a great virtue since the majestic godhead himself condescends to it so readily. Reverence can quickly be transformed into friendship and the person who was distant can be brought close in a moment [. . .]

From the beginning of my conversion [. . .] I have collected all the cares and bitter experiences of my Lord and have always kept them close to my breast. These include, to start with, the privations of his infant years, then, the labours he went through as he preached and travelled everywhere, his waiting on God in prayer, his fasts and temptations, his tears and compassion, the traps that were set for him in discussions, and, last of all, dangers from false brethren, insults, being spat on, beaten, abused, scorned, pierced by nails, and other things, which Christ suffered for the salvation of mankind. All these experiences may be collected up, like wood, from the Gospels. Among all the branches of fragrant myrrh you must not pass over what Christ endured on the cross nor how he was embalmed in the tomb. On the cross Christ dealt with the bitterness of my sins and in the tomb he declared that my body would enjoy immortality.

As long as I live I shall proclaim aloud the abundance of the graces which come from these events. I shall never forget these mercies because I have been restored to life through them [...]

You become wise by meditating on these things. From this meditation comes righteousness, full knowledge, many merits and the riches of salvation. These meditations sometimes include bitter experiences and sometimes the sweet blessings of consolations. In adversities they lift me up and in prosperity they keep a check on my exuberant joy. Between the sadnesses and joys of this life they enable me to walk safely along the royal road that leads to life as I am protected from danger on both sides.

The Judge of the whole world has shown me that Jesus is both gentle and humble. Jesus is not only willing to receive me and to pardon me, but even more, he who is far above all powers has been given to me to be my model to imitate. That is why I so frequently talk about the sufferings of Jesus, as you know, and why they are always in my heart, as God knows. Jesus's sufferings are the constant theme of all my writings, as is well known. In a word, my philosophy is this, and it is the highest one in the world: to know Jesus and him crucified [...]

You must have Jesus constantly before your eyes. Then you will see clearly the pains that the Lord endured for you and you will then willingly bear your own pains through his help. Jesus is the Bridegroom of the Church and is above all. May God be blessed forever. Amen.

From Sermon 43 on the Song of Songs, tr. S. Eales (1895), in H. Backhouse (ed.), *The Song of Songs: Selections from the Sermons of St Bernard of Clairvaux* (Hodder & Stoughton, London, 1990).

QUESTIONS TO PONDER

1. 'Reverence can quickly be transformed into friendship.' Bernard interprets the Song of Songs as an allegory of the spiritual marriage and union between Christ the Bridegroom and the soul/Church, the Bride. What are the strengths – and dangers – of this image of spiritual intimacy with God?
2. 'I have collected all the cares and bitter experiences of my Lord.' Bernard shares how he relates the events of Christ's incarnation to his own life. How can we connect with the events Bernard mentions, so that they are not distant, but touch our experiences today?
3. 'These meditations sometimes include bitter experiences and sometimes the sweet blessings of consolation.' How does meditation affect you? In what ways can our own hurts – and joys – become transformed and changed by being identified with Christ's?

PRESENT WITH YOU OR
ABSENT. NOTHING.

4. 'You will then willingly bear your own pains.' Reflect on the different ways in which we can relate to the cross of Jesus in prayer, for example, in confession, adoration, intercession. How can the cross help us to find meaning and hope in our own sufferings?
5. Medieval Christians focused on the cross of Christ in a time of many mortal dangers. How can contemplation of the passion be kept within the perspective of the Easter victory of Christ? What imbalances could result in our prayers if we lost this perspective? See Galatians 2.20.

PRAYER EXERCISE

Either:
Create a collage, in words or in pictures, of episodes from the life of Christ that particularly speak to you. Reflect on why you have chosen these ones. What other events could inspire your life-situation? Give thanks.

Or:
Pray before a cross or crucifix. Spend some time in adoration, confession, intercession, thanksgiving. Place votive candles (night-lights) around the cross to represent people or situations to be enfolded within Christ's passion, as symbols of hope.

FOR FURTHER READING

Leclercq, J., *Bernard of Clairvaux and the Cistercian Spirit*. Cistercian Publications, Michigan, 1980.
Merton, T., *Merton on St Bernard*. Cistercian Publications, Michigan, 1980.

The 13th Century:
Francis of Assisi

THE THIRTEENTH CENTURY saw a continuing shift of focus from the monasteries to the expanding cities as centres of culture and study. Episcopal schools, alongside the cathedrals, had been growing since the time of Charlemagne, and had been further encouraged by the reforms of Pope Gregory VII, but now independent universities came into existence – for example at Paris, Oxford and Cambridge. Renewed interest in Aristotle's philosophy led to the exploration of the relationship of reason and revelation – the educational method called 'Scholasticism' begun by Anselm was now developed in the work of Thomas Aquinas (1225–74). His *Summa Theologica* sought to defend orthodox Christian beliefs within the framework of a philosophy acceptable to the intellectual thinkers of the age. Thomas himself was a member of the Order of Preachers founded by Dominic in 1220.

The contrasting figures of Dominic and Francis pioneered a Christian lifestyle and discipleship that united the goal of apostolic mission with a fundamental commitment to poverty – the mendicant (or begging) friars. Dominic's order was dedicated to preaching and study, and his friars became established at most university towns, contributing greatly to research, learning and debate.

✠

FRANCIS (1181–1226) turned his back on his well-to-do family at Assisi, first interpreting literally his call to 'rebuild my Church' by repairing the ruined chapel of San Damiano. But it was to a restoration of the Church to the gospel values of simplicity and generosity that Francis was being summoned, realized when he heard read the words of Matthew 10.7–9. Early on, he chanced to meet on the road a leper – who, with his sores and disfigurements, was one of the most despised and feared of society. Francis found himself constrained to dismount his horse, to reach out to the leper, touch and embrace him – then he was gone! Had Francis encountered Christ? His heart s changed, and he found a new resolve to draw close to the world's untouchables and to love Christ present in them.

He soon gathered an ever-growing band of followers prepared for this radical commitment to poverty and evangelism, while St Clare led a similar society for women. His journeys led him to Rome, Spain, Eastern Europe and Egypt. Retiring to Mt Alverna in 1224, he received the gift of the stigmata, the wounds of Christ appearing on his hands and feet.

In contrast to the remote location of the Cistercian monasteries, the Franciscans, like the Dominicans, came to establish lodges close to where people lived, worked and studied. These friaries as places of welcome and counsel in the cities complemented the itinerant ministries of the brothers throughout the countryside. Franciscan spirituality was, and is, characterized by a deep love for Christ and his cross, by a delight in creation and by a desire to integrate the experience of prayer into a life of service. The Rule of 1221 represents an early attempt to describe such values for the emerging Order.

A Reading from Francis of Assisi

The friars should be delighted to follow the lowliness and poverty of our Lord Jesus Christ, remembering that of the whole world we must own nothing; 'but having food and sufficient clothing, with these let us be content' (1 Timothy 6.8), as St Paul says. They should be glad to live among social outcasts, among the poor and helpless, the sick and the lepers, and those who beg by the wayside. If they are in want, they should not be ashamed to beg alms, remembering that our Lord Jesus Christ, the Son of the living, all-powerful God 'set his face like a very hard rock' (Isaiah 50.7) and was not ashamed. He was poor and he had no home of his own and he lived on alms, he and the Blessed Virgin and his disciples [. . .]

The friars should have no hesitation about telling one another what they need, so that they can provide for one another. They are bound to love and care for one another as brothers, according to the means God gives them, just as a mother loves and cares for her son [. . .]

Remember the words of our Lord, 'Love your enemies, do good to those who hate you' (Matthew 5.44). Our Lord Jesus Christ himself, in whose footsteps we must follow (cf. 1 Peter 2.21), called the man who betrayed him his friend, and gave himself up of his own accord to his executioners. Therefore, our friends are those who for no reason cause us trouble and suffering, shame or injury, pain or torture, even martyrdom and death. It is these we must love, and love very much, because for all they do to us we are given eternal life [...]

We have left the world now and all we have to do is to be careful to obey God's will and please him. We must be very careful, or we will turn out to be like the earth by the wayside, or the stony or thorn-choked ground, as our Lord tells us in the Gospel (Luke 8.11–15) [...] We should beware especially of the malice and wiles of Satan; his only desire is to prevent man from raising his mind and heart to his Lord and God [...] By the anxieties and worries of this life he tries to dull man's heart and make a dwelling for himself there [...] And so we must all keep close watch over ourselves or we will be lost and turn our minds and hearts from God, because we think there is something worth having or doing, or that we will gain some advantage. /

In that love which is God (cf. 1 John 4.16), I entreat all my friars, ministers and subjects, to put away every attachment, all care and solicitude, and serve, love, honour, and adore our Lord and God with a pure heart and mind; this is what he seeks above all else. We should make a dwelling-place within ourselves where he can stay, he who is the Lord God almighty, Father, Son, and Holy Spirit.

From *The Rule of 1221*, chapters 9 and 22, in M. A. Habig (ed.), *St Francis of Assisi: Writings and Early Biographies: English Omnibus of Sources for the Life of St Francis* (Franciscan Herald Press, Chicago, 1973).

QUESTIONS TO PONDER

1. 'With these let us be content.' We may not be called to poverty but we are called to simplicity of lifestyle, travelling light in a spirit of joyful thankfulness and trustfulness. What does this mean for life today? How can we simplify the way we live?

2. 'We must be very careful.' Francis calls us to watchfulness, and identifies some of the dangers along the pathway. What pressures from society must we resist today?

3. 'Glad to live among social outcasts.' Who are today's lepers? In what sort of ways is it possible to live in solidarity with the marginalized who may be some distance from our homes, and overseas? How does the Gospel, especially Matthew 25.35–41, shape our attitudes and reactions? How can the way we live show support?

4. Are there people around us who 'cause us pain and suffering'? How can our prayer lead us to respond to them differently? Can we be agents of reconciliation in our own community?

5. 'This is what he seeks above all else.' Part of the secret of simplicity is single-heartedness, discovering an overarching vision and priority in life which gives unity and meaning to all our different activities. How would you express the main focus of your lifestyle?

PRAYER EXERCISE

Either:

Read Luke 12.22–34. Silently make a review of your own lifestyle in the light of these directives. What is important in life, and what is not? Conclude with the Franciscan prayer idea, holding your arms out wide to make the shape of the cross in your body, and surrender your resolves to Christ.

Or:

Rewrite – even enact – the parable of the Good Samaritan (Luke 10.25–37) in modern terms. Who is today's victim, who the passers-by, who the helper? Conclude with prayers for those who are cast down today throughout the world, reflecting on your own response.

FOR FURTHER READING

Foster, R., *Freedom of Simplicity*. Triangle, London, 1981.

Sider, R. J., *Rich Christians in An Age of Hunger*. Hodder & Stoughton, London, 1990.

Stoutzenberger, J. M. and Bohrer, J. D., *Praying with Francis of Assisi*. Saint Mary's Press, Minnesota, 1989.

The 14ᵗʰ Century:
Julian of Norwich

THE FOURTEENTH CENTURY was a time of deep distress in the Church and beyond, but also witnessed a remarkable flowering of spirituality in Greece, along the Rhine, and in England.

The Western Church was unsettled by the removal of the seat of the papacy to Avignon in France, and by a forty-year period of schism when a rival pope was elected in 1378. Such divisiveness led John Wycliffe (1330–84), a theologian from Oxford, to try to recover and promote a more scriptural view of the Church. He maintained a powerful critique of the weaknesses of the institutional church, and sought to identify the elements of 'true Church' – a body of people who have Christ as their head. Perhaps Wycliffe's greatest achievement was encouraging the first-ever English translation of the Scriptures, though English Bibles were to be officially banned in 1407!

Europe was devastated by the bubonic plague which raged from 1348. The 'Black Death' killed about one third of the population, robbing churches of their pastors and leaders, and leading to a new focus on the passion and death of Christ in popular prayer, and a fear of the wrath of God.

But it was during this period that, in different parts of the world, there bubbled up the new springs of a hopeful spirituality. In Greece, new monasteries flourished on Mount Athos, representing almost the whole Orthodox world, as monks came from Russia, Serbia, Bulgaria and beyond. Among the outstanding teachers of prayer that emerged in the fourteenth century were St Gregory of Sinai and St Gregory Palamas. Their search for stillness in prayer, *hesychia*, led to the use of the Jesus Prayer, 'Lord Jesus Christ, Son of God, have mercy on me a sinner', as a tool for uniting mind and heart in contemplation. In Germany, a succession of spiritual teachers known collectively as the Rhineland Mystics began with Meister Eckhart (1260–1327). In powerful and direct writing he stressed humanity's capacity for union with the transcendent Creator, but he was accused of the heresy of overstating the affinity between God and the soul.

An England fraught by the double horrors of disease and war produced spiritual writings which reveal a deep thirst for the God who never changes, the God beyond. The anonymous *Cloud of Unknowing* describes prayer as entering a darkness where concepts fail, where we need to go beyond words and reach God by longing and loving, not by thinking. Walter Hilton maps out the spiritual journey in his *Ladder of Ascent*, while Richard Rolle depicts prayer as the 'Fire of Love' in the soul leading to the 'breakthrough' of knowledge when one is 'aware of a heavenly secret infused into his sweet love, and known only by himself'.

JULIAN of Norwich (c. 1342–1416) stands within this English mystical tradition. Living as a hermit in a little cell attached to a parish church, she experienced a series of vivid revelations when she was thirty. She composed her *Showings* some twenty years later, and they contain the fruit of her reflections on what she had discovered about God. While she glimpses immense suffering in the heart of God as seen on the cross, her vision of the divine is supremely optimistic, celebrating a God whose love can conquer all human weaknesses. Her God is both awesome and tender, 'courteous and homely'. Prayer is the meeting point between human longings and God's own desire to reveal himself, and God delights in the heart that is turned towards him with humility and expectancy.

A Reading from Julian of Norwich

Our good Lord showed [me] a spiritual sight of his familiar love. I saw that he is to us everything which is good and comforting for our help. He is our clothing, who wraps and enfolds us for love, embraces us and shelters us, surrounds us for his love, which is so tender that he may never desert us. And so in this sight I saw that he is everything which is good, as I understand.

And in this he showed me something small, no bigger than a hazelnut, lying in the palm of my hand, as it seemed to me, and it was as round as a ball. I looked at it with the eye of my understanding and thought: What can this be? I was amazed that it could last, for I thought that because of its littleness it would suddenly have fallen into nothing. And I was answered in my understanding: It lasts and always will, because God loves it; and thus everything has being through the love of God.

In this little thing I saw three properties. The first is that God made it, the second is that God loves it, the third is that God preserves it. But what did I see in it? It is that God is the Creator and the protector and the lover. For until I am substantially united to him, I can never have perfect rest or true happiness, until, that is, I am so attached to him that there can be no created thing between my God and me [. . .]

I understand three ways of contemplating motherhood in God. The first is the foundation of our nature's creation; the second is his taking of our nature, where the motherhood of grace begins; the third is the motherhood at work [. . .] This fair lovely word 'mother' is so sweet and so kind in itself that it cannot truly be said of anyone or to anyone except of him and to him who is the true Mother of life and of all things [. . .]

And in our spiritual bringing to birth he uses more tenderness, without any comparison, in protecting us. By so much as our soul is more precious in his sight, he kindles our understanding, he prepares our ways, he eases our conscience, he comforts our soul, he illumines our heart and gives us partial knowledge and love of his blessed divinity, with gracious memory of his sweet humanity and his blessed Passion, with courteous wonder over his great surpassing goodness, and makes us to love everything which he loves for love of him, and to be well satisfied with him and with all his works. And when we fall, quickly he raises us up with his loving embrace and his gracious touch. And when we are strengthened by his sweet working, then we willingly choose him by his grace, and we shall be his servants and his lovers, constantly and forever [. . .]

Our Lord is most glad and joyful because of our prayer; and he expects it, and he wants to have it, for with his grace it makes us like to himself in condition as we are in nature, and such is his blessed will. For he says: Pray wholeheartedly, though it seems to you that this has no savour for you; still it is profitable enough, though you may not feel that. Pray wholeheartedly, though you feel nothing, yes, though you think that you could not, for in dryness and in barrenness, in sickness and in weakness, then is your prayer most pleasing to me, though you think it almost tasteless to you. And so is all your living prayer in my sight.

From *Showings*, excerpts from chs 5, 59, 60, 61, 41, in E. Colledge and J. Walsh (trs), *Julian of Norwich: Showings* (Paulist Press Inc., Mahwah, NJ, 1978).

QUESTIONS TO PONDER

1. 'He is everything that is good.' Recall experiences when God has spoken to you through the things of nature. How can we train ourselves to see God in

all things, and at the same time allow 'no created thing between my God and me'?

2. '[. . .] contemplating motherhood in God'. Julian boldly pioneers the idea of the feminine in God. Join her in exploring the various ways Jesus can be mother to us. How do these ideas enrich and balance your understanding of God?
3. 'In sickness and in weakness [. . .] is your prayer most pleasing to me.' Julian prayed in an age of disease and death, and was familiar with illness. What is your experience of praying in weakness, even in dryness and barrenness? Can our vulnerability lead us into a deeper relationship with God? How can we pray when we do not feel like it?
4. Julian could not conceive of anger or wrath in God, only compassion and love. Is her view balanced biblically, too soft, or just right?
5. Julian was above everything a person of hope and confidence in God. Underline parts of the text which express such hope and trust. How do they help you?

PRAYER EXERCISE

Either:
Reflect on and celebrate ways in which God's love surrounds and sustains us. Write intercessions on pieces of paper and place them at the centre of a cloth. Slowly and gently enfold these prayers in the cloth, and perhaps place before a cross, while reading the first paragraph above. Conclude with thanksgivings, using Psalm 130.

Or:
Hold in the palm of your hand a flower, shell, or something from creation – even a hazelnut! Using the 'eyes of your understanding' reflect on its beauty and on its fragility. Let it speak to you of your life precious in God's hands. Read Psalm 8 and give thanks.

FOR FURTHER READING

Jantzen, G., *Julian of Norwich: Mystic and Theologian*. SPCK, London, 1987.
Llewelyn, R., *With Pity Not with Blame*. Darton, Longman & Todd, London, 1982.

The 15th Century:
Thomas à Kempis

THE FIFTEENTH CENTURY saw changes to the political landscape that were deeply to affect the life of the Church. The Byzantine empire fell when the Turks captured Constantinople in 1453, the Muslim Sultan entering the basilica of Holy Wisdom in triumph, the Christian emperor slain defending the city walls. The city was to be renamed Istanbul and become capital to an expanding empire that was to last almost five hundred years. Many churches were turned into mosques, and the centre of influence in Orthodoxy shifted in many ways towards the Russian church, Moscow claiming the title 'the third Rome'. Meanwhile in Europe, new monarchies in England, France and Spain consolidated a growing sense of national identity, and nation states, as we know them, took shape.

It was in Italy that the movement later to be called the Renaissance began. This 'rebirth' or rediscovery of classical Greek and Roman sources of art and literature was furthered by the invention of printing mid-century. Now great texts, including those of the Bible and Church Fathers, could be copied and studied widely. Within a generation or two the printing press was to open up enormous possibilities for making known a radical critique of a Church astray. The seeds of the Reformation were already being planted this century with a fresh interest in the Church's biblical and patristic origins during the Renaissance.

✠

THOMAS À KEMPIS (1380–1471) came from a humble family near Cologne. At the age of twelve, he studied in the Netherlands with a group belonging to the 'Brethren of the Common Life' who introduced him to a type of devotional spirituality that influenced him deeply. He became a monk at the start of the century at Zwolle where he was to remain for the rest of his life. It was from here that he exercised a powerful ministry as spiritual director and writer. In *The Imitation of Christ* he describes the inner life of the disciple, in the strong conviction that Christians can profoundly change and reshape their attitudes into a Christlike way of living and reacting.

Thomas was part of an influential movement of spirituality called 'the Modern Devotion'. Its aim was to open up opportunities for spiritual growth beyond the confines of the cloister – to reach ordinary people with the call to a deeper life of prayer through the dissemination of writings and the formation of Christian schools. It wanted to avoid speculative types of prayer and to popularize the basics of discipleship through practical and accessible teaching. First circulated in 1418 and printed in 1471, *The Imitation* was destined to become one of the most widely read devotional works in the world.

A Reading from Thomas à Kempis

'I will hear what the Lord God speaks within me.' Blessed is the soul that hears the Lord speaking within it, and receives comfort from His Word. Blessed are the ears that hear the still, small voice of God, and disregard the whispers of the world. Blessed are the ears that listen to Truth teaching inwardly, and not to voices from the world. Blessed are the eyes that are closed to outward things, but are open to inward things. Blessed are those who enter deeply into inner things, and daily prepare themselves to receive the secrets of heaven [. . .]

CHRIST. I have said, 'Peace I leave with you; My own peace I give you.' [. . .] If you listen to Me, and follow My words, you shall find true peace. THE DISCIPLE. What must I do, Lord? CHRIST. Keep guard over your whole life, your actions and words. Direct all your efforts to the single purpose of pleasing Me: seek and desire Myself alone [. . .] Do not hold an exaggerated opinion of yourself, or believe that you are a favourite of God when you enjoy the grace of great devotion and sweetness; for it is not by these things that the true lover of holiness is known, or is a man's spiritual progress dependent on such things. THE DISCIPLE. Lord, on what then does it depend? CHRIST. On complete surrender of your heart to the will of God, not seeking to have your own way either in great matters or small, in time or in eternity. If you will make this surrender, you will thank God with equal gladness both in good times and in bad, and will accept everything, as from His hand, with an untroubled mind [. . .]

CHRIST. Naked I hung on the Cross with arms outstretched, offering Myself freely to God the Father for your sins, My whole Person a sacrifice of divine propitiation: you, too, must willingly offer yourself daily to Me in the Eucharist with all your powers and affections as a pure and holy offering [...] I offered Myself wholly to the Father for you: I have given My very Body and Blood to be your food, that I may be all yours, and that you may be mine for ever [...]

THE DISCIPLE. Lord, all things in Heaven and earth are Yours. I desire to give myself to You as a free offering, and to be Yours for ever [...]

Lord, I offer on Your altar of reconciliation all the sins and offences that I have ever committed before You [...]

I offer to You also whatever is good in me, though it be little and imperfect, that You may strengthen and hallow it, make it dear and acceptable to You, and raise it continually towards perfection [...]

I offer You also all the holy aspirations of devout persons; the needs of my parents, friends, brothers, sisters, and all who are dear to me; and the needs of all who have desired or asked me to pray and offer the Eucharist for them and theirs, whether living or departed [...]

I offer You also my prayers and the Sacrifice of Peace in particular for those who have in any way injured, grieved or maligned me, or who have done me any kind of harm or hurt; likewise for any whom I have at any time grieved, troubled, injured or offended by word or deed [...]

CHRIST. Blessed is the man who, whenever he celebrates the Eucharist or receives Communion, offers himself to Our Lord as a living sacrifice.

From *The Imitation of Christ*, 3.1, 3.25, 4.8, 4.9, 4.10, in L. Sherley-Price (tr.), *Thomas à Kempis: The Imitation of Christ* (Penguin, Harmondsworth, 1952).

QUESTIONS TO PONDER

1. 'I will hear what the Lord God speaks within me.' What is your experience of hearing the divine voice? Recalling that it was in this century that Joan of Arc was claiming direction by her 'Voices' within, what are the blessings – and dangers – entailed in such listening? What safeguards do we need?

2. 'Blessed are the ears that listen to Truth teaching inwardly, and not to voices from the world.' Do you agree? Are there times when we should listen to 'voices from the world' in our prayers? What kind of voices should we be especially attuned to? (Look up Mark 10.46–52.)

3. 'Daily prepare [...] to receive the secrets of heaven.' What steps can we take to move from a 'talking' kind of prayer to a more receptive kind?

[handwritten:] ? ARE OUR PRAYERS ALWAYS OF THE TALKING KIND

4. In our second paragraph, Christ calls for 'complete surrender of your heart to the will of God'. For Thomas, this is the secret of nurturing a Christlike life. What holds us back? NAME SOME THINGS?

5. The eucharist was central to Thomas's life of discipleship. How important is it in your search for union with Christ? How can you help it become more meaningful and significant?

PRAYER EXERCISE

Either:

Noting how Thomas describes a dialogue between the disciple and Christ, write out a conversation with Jesus. 'What must I do, Lord?' What questions do you want to put to Christ? How would Christ reply? Practise this form of listening and responding in your private prayers, and allow it to lead you into a closer, more open, relationship with Christ.

Or:

Reflect on your experience of the eucharist. Reread the final paragraphs in our extract and consider what you can offer to God in response to the self-offering of Christ on the cross. Place before a cross an empty basket or dish and a cup to represent the vessels of Holy Communion. Write on pieces of paper the sorts of things which Thomas suggests we offer to God in the eucharist. In place of bread and wine, place into these vessels your petitions and gifts and offer them to God in a spirit of trustfulness and thanksgiving.

FOR FURTHER READING

Post, R. R., *The Modern Development: Studies in Medieval and Reformation Thought*. Brill, Leiden, 1968.

Raitt, J. (ed.), *Christian Spirituality: High Middle Ages and Reformation*. Routledge & Kegan Paul, London, 1987.

Cross
Paper
Pencils
Chalice

Reformation and Renewal: into the Modern World

The 16th Century:
Teresa of Avila

THE SIXTEENTH CENTURY witnessed the religious upheaval we call the Reformation. It began on the continent when Martin Luther nailed his ninety-five theses to the door of the Wittenberg's castle church in 1517. At one level this was a protest against the sale of 'indulgences' – promises of remission of time in purgatory – to raise money for the reconstruction of St Peter's Basilica in Rome. But at a deeper level Luther was calling the Church away from medieval distortions of Christianity and back to gospel values. His key conviction was that a person is saved, not by his own merits or achievements, but only by God's grace, as Paul taught (Romans 3.28). The watchword was *sola scriptura, sola fides* – we come to God only through the teaching of the Bible, not traditions, to establish a relationship based on faith, not on works. Later, in Geneva, John Calvin was to systematize this approach in his *Institutes of the Christian Religion.*

In England Henry VIII precipitated the break with Rome in 1534 when he proclaimed himself head of the Church. Reforming ideas from Europe began to influence his Archbishop, Thomas Cranmer, who wrote the first *Book of Common Prayer* in 1549, giving the people a simplified liturgy in their own tongue. Slowly, changes made themselves felt in parishes, as colourful vestments, hangings and statues were removed, and stone altars replaced by simple wooden tables. Elizabeth I handled the reformers cautiously in her Act of Uniformity in 1559, accommodating change while preserving the traditional Catholic order of bishop, priest and deacon.

Alert to the need for the renewal of doctrine and practice, the Catholic Church convened the Council of Trent in this period. The movement later called the 'Counter-Reformation' sought to clarify and defend Catholic teaching and discipline, with the Jesuits, founded by Ignatius Loyola, promoting its ideals.

TERESA of Avila (1515–82) was twenty when she entered the Carmelite Order. She found monastic life tedious and unfulfilling until she experienced a 'second conversion', occasioned by encountering a statue of the suffering Christ, which moved her to new depths of repentance. Reading Augustine's *Confessions*, she recognized Christ calling her to a new commitment. At the age of forty she realized that her mission was to encourage a radical reform of the religious life and to lead people into greater expectancy and fruitfulness in prayer. She went on to establish sixteen convents, latterly with the help of St John of the Cross.

She wrote *The Interior Castle* in 1577, towards the end of her life, and in many ways it is autobiographical. She depicts the soul as a crystal castle of great beauty, Christ dwelling in the innermost chamber, calling the Christian into an ever-deeper realization of his presence. The experience of prayer is described as a progression in awareness of 'His Majesty', as we move from the outer Mansions of humility and self-knowledge, the rooms of talkative prayer filled with busy thinking, towards the inner Mansions of silent, contemplative, receptive prayer where the voice of Christ can be heard.

This is no theoretical book, but springs from Teresa's own experience and struggles. She writes in an often humorous, down-to-earth way, for she knows, only too well, human foibles and temptations. That is the reason that this work, penned originally for nuns, has been enjoyed by generations of ordinary Christians as a practical and inspiring guide to the spiritual life.

A Reading from Teresa of Avila

You will have heard of the wonderful way in which silk is made – a way which no one could invent but God – and how it comes from a kind of seed which looks like tiny peppercorns [. . .] When the warm weather comes, and the mulberry-trees begin to show leaf, this seed starts to take life; until it has this sustenance, on which it feeds, it is as dead. The silkworms feed on the mulberry-leaves until they are full-grown, when people put down twigs, upon which, with their tiny mouths, they start spinning silk, making themselves very tight little cocoons, in which they bury themselves. Then, finally, the worm, which was large and ugly, comes right out of the cocoon a beautiful white butterfly [. . .]

The silkworm is like the soul which takes life when, through the heat which comes from the Holy Spirit, it begins to utilize the general help which God gives to us all, and to make use of the remedies which He left in His Church – such as frequent confessions, good books and sermons, for these are the remedies for a soul dead in negligences and sins and frequently plunged into temptation. The soul begins to live and nourishes itself on this food, and on good meditations, until it is full grown – and this is what concerns me now [. . .]

When it is full-grown, then, [. . .] it starts to spin its silk and to build the house in which it is to die. This house may be understood here to mean Christ. I think I read or heard somewhere that our life is hid in Christ [. . .]

Here, then, daughters, you see what we can do, with God's favour. May His Majesty Himself be our Mansion as He is in this Prayer of Union which, as it were, we ourselves spin [. . .] And, before we have finished doing all that we can in that respect, God will take this tiny achievement of ours, which is nothing at all, unite it with His greatness and give it such worth that its reward will be the Lord Himself [. . .]

On, then, my daughters! Let us hasten to perform this task and spin this cocoon. Let us renounce self-love and self-will, and our attachment to earthly things. Let us practise penance, prayer, mortification, obedience, and all the other good works that you know of. Let us do what we have been taught; and we have been instructed about what our duty is. Let the silkworm die – let it die, as in fact it does when it has completed the work which it was created to do. Then we shall see God and shall ourselves be as completely hidden in His greatness as is this little worm in its cocoon [. . .]

And now let us see what becomes of this silkworm, for all that I have been saying about it is leading up to this. When it is in this state of prayer, and quite dead to the world, it comes out a little white butterfly [. . .] By comparison with the abode it has had, everything it sees on earth leaves it dissatisfied, especially when God has again and again given it this wine which almost every time has brought it some new blessing. It sets no store by the things it did when it was a worm – that is, by its gradual weaving of the cocoon. It has wings now: how can it be content to crawl along slowly when it is able to fly?

From *Interior Castle*, V.ii,
in E. A. Peers (tr.), *St Teresa of Avila: Interior Castle* (Sheed & Ward, London, 1974).

QUESTIONS TO PONDER

1. The Reformation debate centred on the role of God's grace and human efforts, and here Teresa describes prayer as a partnership with God, in which we have a certain part to play, but it is God who brings metamorphosis, inner transformation. What spiritual disciplines does

Teresa commend? What is their role today? How would you explain the place of such 'good works' in building a relationship with God?

2. 'Let us renounce self-love and self-will, and our attachment to earthly things.' Is this the heart of the matter, the most important thing we can do? If so, why?

3. In her image of the silkworm/butterfly Teresa describes the need for death and resurrection in the spiritual life. What do you understand by the words of Paul she alludes to: 'For you have died, and your life is hid with Christ in God' (Colossians 3.3)?

4. Teresa describes the contrast between a period in which our prayer-life is very hidden, God working secretly in us as within a cocoon, when we become almost dead to external stimuli and wrapped up in Christ, and a period when our prayer-life becomes more visible, like a butterfly which is both beautiful and vulnerable – in the *Interior Castle* she goes on to talk of the need for 'a perfect love of neighbour'. How does this correspond to your experience? Do times of withdrawal lead to times of witness? How important is the 'cocoon' stage in the spiritual life?

5. Teresa is teaching, in this 'Mansion' or stage of the spiritual life, about the 'Prayer of Union'. The butterfly-soul 'has wings now: how can it be content to crawl along slowly when it is able to fly?' Into what sort of freedoms does God want to lead us in our prayer-life and discipleship?

PRAYER EXERCISE

Either:

Teresa uses a vivid image to describe God at work in her life. Draw a picture or describe an image or parable to express an important moment or stage in your spiritual experience. Place it before God in a spirit of gratitude.

Or:

Reflect on your discipleship. Have you known Teresa's experience of spiritual breakthrough, or are you at a 'cocoon' stage? Is it time to find wings, to fly? Take time to give thanks that God is uniquely at work in your individuality. Do not compare yourself with others, but do ask God to lead you forwards in the adventure of prayer.

FOR FURTHER READING

Bielecki, T., *Teresa of Avila: An Introduction to Her Life and Writings*. Burns & Oates, Tunbridge Wells, 1994.

Humpheys, C., *From Ash to Fire: A Contemporary Journey through the Interior Castle of Teresa of Avila*. New City Press, New York, 1992.

The 17th Century:
John Bunyan

THE SEVENTEENTH CENTURY witnessed the redrawing of the religious map in the wake of the Reformation, and the emergence of distinctive elements within Protestantism, the origins of later separate denominations.

While the Mediterranean countries remained mainly Catholic, and Scandinavia and the Netherlands embraced Protestantism, central Europe became a battleground both ideologically and literally. The Thirty Years' War (1618–48) became a bitter struggle between Catholics and Calvinists, ending in a compromise treaty which urged peaceful coexistence.

In England, James I succeeded Elizabeth and gave encouragement to a new translation of the Bible – the Authorized Version published in 1611. But he continued Elizabeth's intolerance of the Puritans. They were determined to 'purify' the English church of anything resembling Catholic practice, and to bring it a deeper reformation on Calvin's Geneva model. Wanting to change the Church from within, they became alienated and found themselves forming separate congregations, the precursor of the congregationalist churches. As many as twenty thousand were to emigrate to the New World, the first 'Pilgrim Fathers' setting out in the *Mayflower* in 1620.

Other dissenting bodies emerged during this century: Baptists, promoting adult baptism and influenced by radical continental thinking; Quakers, encouraging individual religious experience, led by George Fox; and the Presbyterians, unsuccessful in trying to rid the English Church of bishops but becoming the established church in Scotland. It was not until the Toleration Act of 1689 that these groups began to win official recognition in England and the right to build chapels. Before then, they had suffered hard in the turbulent years of civil war in England when the High Churchman Charles I sought to rid his kingdom of Calvinists. After his execution in 1649, Puritans came to prominence under Oliver Cromwell but became marginalized under Charles II. His Act of Uniformity in 1662 established the use of a version of the *Book of Common Prayer* still in use today, but drove out of the Church of England those who would not conform – the 'Nonconformists'.

✠

JOHN BUNYAN (1628–88) found himself caught up in these events. The son of a tinker, he became a soldier in the Parliamentary Army in the 1650s. These were years of intense spiritual struggle for Bunyan, who tried to change his life outwardly without having an inner experience of Christ. His conversion in about 1655 was a major turning point, and he became a preacher for the congregation of Independents in Bedford. He was gaoled for some twelve years during the persecution of Charles II, and began his first books during the imprisonment, *Grace Abounding* appearing in 1666.

After his release, he went back to preach for the Bedford congregation and began an evangelistic ministry which took him further afield. He wrote *Pilgrim's Progress* in 1678, reflecting something of his own eventful spiritual journey.

A Reading from John Bunyan

As I walked through the wilderness of the world, I came to a place where there was a den. There I lay down to sleep; and as I slept, I dreamed a dream. In my dream I saw a man clothed with rags, standing by a path with a book in his hand and a great burden upon his back [. . .]

Christian finally came to the little gate. Over the gate was written, in bold letters: 'KNOCK, AND IT SHALL BE OPENED UNTO YOU.' Christian knocked [. . .] At last one came to the gate whose name was Goodwill. He asked, in a deep voice, 'Who's there, where did you come from, and what do you want?'

CHRISTIAN: I am a poor, burdened sinner. I come from the City of Destruction, and I want to go to Mount Zion, that I may be safe from the coming wrath of God. I am informed that through this gate is the way to Zion. I would like to know, therefore, if you will let me in.

GOODWILL: [. . .] We do not reject any who come. No matter what they have done before coming, they are in no wise cast out. And now, my good pilgrim, come with me a little way, and I will show you the way to go. Now look yonder. Do you see that narrow way? That is the road you must take. It was travelled by the patriarchs in olden times, and by the prophets, and by Christ and His apostles; and it is as straight as a line can make it.

CHRISTIAN: But are there no turnings or windings by which a stranger may lose his way?

GOODWILL: Yes, there are many roads branching off from this one, but you can distinguish the right way from the wrong, for the right way is the only road that is straight and narrow.

Then Christian asked Mr Goodwill if he would remove the burden from his back, for he was still carrying it and could by no means get it off without help. Goodwill counselled: 'Be content to bear your burden a little longer, until you come to the place of deliverance. Then it will fall from your shoulders of itself.' Now Christian began to prepare for his journey [...]

Now I saw in my dream Christian walking briskly up a highway fenced on both sides with a high wall. He began to run, though he could not run fast because of the load on his back. On top of the hill, he came to a cross. Just as he got to the cross, his burden came loose, dropped from his shoulders, and went tumbling down the hill. It fell into an open grave, and I saw it no more.

Now Christian's heart was light. He had found relief from his burden. He said to himself, 'He has given me rest by His sorrows, and life by His death.' He stood gazing at the cross, wondering how the sight of the cross could so relieve one of guilt and shame [...] He was so thankful [...]

[...] At a great distance, Christian could see a magnificent mountainous country. In this faraway land were great forests, green vineyards, sparkling fountains, broad fields [...] He asked the name of the country. They said, 'It is Immanuel's Land, and it is for all pilgrims, just as this hill is, and from there you will be able to see the gate of the Celestial City, as the shepherds there will show you.'

He expressed his desire to go, and they were willing. 'But first,' they suggested, 'let us go again to the armoury.' There they equipped him from head to foot with what he would need most in his journey. Being thus clothed, he walked out with his friends to the gate [...]

At the foot of the hill, Christian's good companions gave him a loaf of bread, a bottle of wine, and a large bunch of raisins. Bidding them goodbye, he went on alone.

From *The Pilgrim's Progress*, chs 1, 2, 3,
in J. H. Thomas, *The Pilgrim's Progress in Today's English* (Victory Press,
Eastbourne, 1972).

QUESTIONS TO PONDER

1. In Christian's journey to the City of God, Bunyan develops a rich biblical image. God calls Abraham to step out in faith (Genesis 12.1–9); Moses leads the Israelites out of slavery, through the wilderness towards the promised land. In his Gospel, Mark depicts Jesus going on ahead of the disciples to lead them to the cross and beyond (10.32). The first Christians were called 'people of the Way' (Acts 9.2; cf. John 14.6). Paul loves the metaphor of moving forward (Galatians 5.16; Philippians 3.12). How can the idea of spiritual journey/pilgrimage/adventure inspire our understanding about relating to God?

2. 'There are many roads branching off from this one.' On his journey, Christian comes to several junctions where he must make a choice about the direction to take. How does your faith inform the decisions you must make, when you find yourself at a crossroads?

3. In his trek, Christian encounters rough terrain, places of temptation and trial, and people who would sidetrack him – with names like 'Ignorance', 'Talkative' and 'Superstition'. But God provides companions to bring him through – friends Bunyan calls 'Hopeful', 'Faithful'. How can we, as a pilgrim people, support one another more effectively in the spiritual journey? What forms of encouragement can you give – and receive – from others?

4. 'Christian's good companions gave him a loaf of bread, a bottle of wine.' What provisions does God give us for the spiritual journey? How can we make better use of them?

5. Have you been on a pilgrimage of some sort? How can holy places inspire us?

PRAYER EXERCISE

Either:

Reflect on your faith-journey. On a piece of paper draw a time-line, with decades marked off 0 to 100 (!). Above the line put a plus sign (+) to indicate positive moments and below the line place a minus sign (−) where there has been a difficult period. Thank God for the people who have helped you on your pilgrimage, led you into faith or deepened your commitment. Look forward in hope by writing on a card a target or objective for your life of discipleship for the next twelve months. Make your goal challenging but realistic. Surrender this to God by placing your card before a cross in silent trust. Close by reading the last paragraph of our extract.

Or:

Jesus urged his disciples to travel light and be single-minded in their journey (Matthew 10.5–10). Place before you a cross. Read Matthew 11.28–30. Take a stone in your hand and feel its weight. Let it represent a burden you are carrying, a concern that weighs heavily upon you. Prayerfully place it at the foot of the cross. Let go of your worry and yield it to God. Read the third paragraph of our extract, and join Christian in giving thanks. Re-commit yourself to walking forward with Christ.

For Further Reading

Bunyan, J., *Prayer.* Banner of Truth Trust, London, 1965.

Nuttall, G. F., *The Puritan Spirit.* Epworth, London, 1967.

Wakefield, G. S., *Puritan Devotion.* Epworth, London, 1957.

For the 'time-line' idea in the prayer exercise see Council of Churches for Britain and Ireland, *Hope in a Time of Change.* CCBI, London, 1997.

The 18th Century:
John Wesley

THE EIGHTEENTH CENTURY was a time when a sense of spiritual emptiness and need opened the door to an unprecedented revival springing up in different places. In Germany, Lutheranism's descent into a dry orthodoxy – a sort of 'Protestant Scholasticism' – was met by a recovery of devotion and commitment in the Pietist revival, pioneered by Philip Spener, which emphasized the necessity of a new birth and personal faith. Spener's godson Count Zinzendorf helped to establish a Moravian community at Herrnhut near Dresden which sent missionaries to England in the 1720s.

John and Charles Wesley first met the Moravians on a voyage to Georgia. The brothers, both Anglican priests, were on a mission to New England but their own spiritual experience was dim. They were struck by the Moravians' warmth of devotion, and on their return John sought them out again, making a pilgrimage to Herrnhut to discover their secret. He was urged to set aside his own efforts at salvation and rely on Christ's grace alone. In May 1738 Wesley had a conversion experience that was to redirect his life.

From now on, he was determined to bring an evangelistic message of repentance to the people of England, whose religious commitment was so shallow. He rode thousands of miles on horseback to address vast open-air meetings, and followed these up by having local 'class meetings' organized for the continuing instruction and fellowship of believers. Originally within the Church of England, they were to become the origins of the new movement of Methodism.

England's 'Evangelical Revival' was born, while the American colonies experienced their own 'Awakening', Wesley's colleague the great preacher George Whitefield going over to build on the foundations begun by Jonathan Edwards (1703–58). Both these movements resulted in new dedication to missionary enterprise, competing with powerful Catholic missions which had begun earlier with the explorations into the 'New World'. Missionaries followed traders and colonists into undiscovered lands, Catholics establishing missions as far-flung as Latin America and China, Evangelicals beginning their efforts on the continent of Africa.

But this century was to see a deep questioning of the Christian faith which would shake the churches to the core. The Enlightenment produced a generation of influential thinkers who questioned the foundations of faith in their search for a rational explanation for everything. Reason and logic were their yardsticks. In France, the seeds sown by people like Voltaire were to germinate in the violent overthrow of the *ancien régime* in the Revolution of 1789. Meanwhile, in Britain, the Industrial Revolution was to change for ever both the physical and ideological landscape, creating unforeseen new challenges and opportunities for the churches.

✠

JOHN WESLEY (1703–91) was not only a courageous preacher, but also an articulate theologian. His search for an authentic, consistent Christian experience began in his university days at Oxford, where he tried to work out a 'method' or plan of spiritual disciplines, and found inspiration in the early Church Fathers and in later mystics like Thomas à Kempis. We have seen how his personal quest led him to an awareness of deep inner need, and prompted a new look at the Scriptures. At a time when spiritual mediocrity and superficiality were commonplace, he became insistent on the necessity of a continuing repentance to allow God to make radical changes in the heart of men and women. He expressed these ideas, sometimes controversially, in his doctrine of 'Christian perfection' or 'Scriptural holiness'.

A Reading from John Wesley

Perhaps the general prejudice against Christian Perfection may chiefly arise from a misunderstanding about its nature. We willingly allow, and continually declare, that there is no such thing as a perfection in this life that implies either a dispensation from doing good, and observing all the ordinances of God, or a freedom from ignorance, mistake, temptation, and a thousand weaknesses which are necessarily connected with flesh and blood [. . .]

But whom then do you mean by 'one that is perfect'? We mean one in whom is 'the mind which was in Christ', and who so 'walks as Christ also walked'; a man 'who has clean hands and a pure heart' (Psalm 24.4), or who is 'purified from everything that contaminates body and spirit' (see 2 Corinthians 7.1), one in whom 'there is nothing to make his brother stumble' (see 1 John 2.10), and who, accordingly, 'cannot go on sinning' ['he cannot sin' AV] (1 John 3.9).

To explain this in a little more detail: we understand that the scriptural expression, 'become mature' ['a perfect man' AV] (Ephesians 4.13), refers to the person in whom God has fulfilled his faithful word, 'you will be clean; I will cleanse you from all your impurities and from all your idols' (Ezekiel 36.25). We understand from this one whom God has made holy throughout in body, soul, and spirit; one who 'walks in the light, as he is in the light, in whom there is no darkness at all; the blood of Jesus, his Son, having purified him from all sin' (see 1 John 1.7, 5).

This man can now testify to all mankind, 'I have been crucified with Christ and I no longer live, but Christ lives in me' (Galatians 2.20). He 'is holy as God who called him is holy' both in heart and 'in all he does' (see 1 Peter 1.15–16). He 'loves the Lord his God with all his heart', serves him 'with all his strength'. He 'loves his neighbour', every man, 'as himself' (see Luke 10.27) [. . .] Indeed his soul is all love, filled with 'compassion, kindness, humility, gentleness and patience' (Colossians 3.12). And his life agrees with this, being full of 'work produced by faith, labour prompted by love, and endurance inspired by hope' (see 1 Thessalonians 1.3). 'And whatever he does, whether in word or deed', he does 'it all in the name', in the love and power, 'of the Lord Jesus' (see Colossians 3.17). In a word, he does 'the will of God on earth, as it is done in heaven' (see Matthew 6.10).

This is what it is to be a perfect man, for God has 'made perfect for ever those who are being made holy' (Hebrews 10.14), even 'to have a heart so all-flaming with the love of God' (to use Archbishop Usher's words) 'as continually to offer up every thought, word, and work, as a spiritual sacrifice, acceptable to God through Jesus Christ' (see 1 Peter 2.5) [. . .] In other words, to be inwardly and outwardly devoted to God; all devoted in heart and life.

Lord, I believe, thy work of grace
Is perfect in the soul!
His heart is pure who sees thy face,
His spirit is made whole [. . .]

He walks in glorious liberty,
To sin entirely dead;
The Truth, the Son hath made him free,
And he is free indeed.

Throughout his soul thy glories shine,
His soul is all renew'd,
And deck'd in righteousness divine,
And clothed and fill'd with God.

This is the rest, the life, the peace,
Which all thy people prove;
Love is the bond of perfectness,
And all their soul is love [. . .]

Come, O my God, thyself reveal,
Fill all this mighty void;
Thou only canst my spirit fill;
Come, O my God, my God!

From the Preface to Charles and John Wesley's *Hymns*, Vol. 3, in H. C. Backhouse (ed.), *A Plain Man's Guide to Holiness: Wesley's Plain Account of Christian Perfection* (Hodder & Stoughton, London, 1988).

QUESTIONS TO PONDER

1. 'Come O my God, thyself reveal, Fill all this mighty void.' Is awareness of need the prerequisite of personal and corporate revival? In what ways can a sense of spiritual dissatisfaction be a good thing?
2. Wesley was concerned to describe a perfect Christian. How adequate do you find his account? What words or biblical ideas would you use to depict the goals of holiness and spiritual maturity?
3. A key passage for Wesley was Philippians 2.1–13, especially the phrases 'the mind of Christ' and 'work out your own salvation with fear and trembling; for God is at work in you'. What do you think Paul means by these words?
4. 'Inwardly and outwardly devoted to God.' What steps can we take to maintain a consistent Christian life? How can we fulfil in our working lives in a secular world the injunction 'Whatever you do, in word or deed, do everything in the name of the Lord Jesus' (Colossians 3.17)? How can the offering up of 'every thought, word, and work' transform ordinary tasks?
5. 'And all their soul is love.' For Wesley, the heart of the matter of Christian perfection was 'perfect love'. In what sense could it be true 'love is all we need'? Compare the two Great Commandments in Luke 10.27.

PRAYER EXERCISE

Either:

For fifty-five years, Wesley kept a daily journal in which he recorded his spiritual progress – and setbacks. Famously, in his entry for 24 May 1738 he relates his conversion in the words: 'In the evening I went very unwillingly to a society in Aldersgate Street, where one was reading Luther's *Preface* to the Epistle to the Romans. About a quarter before nine, while he was describing the change which God works in the heart through faith in Christ, I felt my heart strangely warmed. I felt I did trust in Christ, Christ alone for salvation; and an assurance was given me that He had taken away *my* sins, even *mine*.' Consider beginning a spiritual journal for yourself, allowing time for daily self-examination and reflection on God's work in your life. Start now by penning the story of your conversion – write out your 'testimony' of discovering Christ.

Or:

John's brother Charles wrote over 5,500 hymns, powerfully expressing both doctrine and experience, and they played an important part in the Evangelical Revival. Take a hymnbook and checking the index of authors, choose one that is used today. How does it help you? Sing it!

FOR FURTHER READING

Alexander, D. A. (ed.), *Christian Spirituality: Five Views of Sanctification*. Inter Varsity Press, Illinois, 1988.

Packer, J. I., *Keep in Step with the Spirit*. Inter Varsity Press, Leicester, 1984.

ihc

The *19*th Century:
John Henry Newman

THE NINETEENTH CENTURY called the Church to a fresh outworking of its faith and to a rethinking of its mission. Industrialization created new forms of poverty and exploitation, while scientific advances and Darwin's theory of evolution posed questions demanding a fresh defence of Christian belief. In the wake of the Enlightenment period and the French Revolution, there was a new freedom to criticize ancient 'givens', and philosophers opened up secular and materialist 'world-views' that needed no God.

The churches responded on all fronts. In France, Catholics recovered some ground lost in the vicious period of anti-clericalism, and witnessed a remarkable flowering of religious orders. The loss of the Papal States in Italy led to a new defensiveness and the Vatican Council called in 1869 redefined the papacy in terms of an 'infallible' authority in spiritual matters, and attempted to quell the rising tide of liberalism. Meanwhile, in the Orthodox world, the Russian church was inextricably bound up with the ruling monarchy of the Tsars. The nineteenth century saw a revival of spirituality through the ministry of spiritual guides called *startsy*, encouraged by the famous *starets* Seraphim of Sarov, while the anonymous *The Way of a Pilgrim* popularized more widely the use of the Jesus Prayer.

In England, new forms of biblical scholarship brought a fresh science to the study of the New Testament, researchers like Westcott at Cambridge exploring the historical background and origins of texts to bring a new confidence in exegesis. Slowly, middle-class churches of scholars and preachers woke up to the pastoral problems of rapid urbanization. In addition to vast new church buildings, missions began to appear that responded to the needs of both body and soul. Evangelicals like William Wilberforce and Lord Shaftesbury fought for slavery abolition and factory reform in parliament and missions like the Salvation Army gradually moved from revivalist origins into the arena of social welfare. At home, the churches pioneered new provisions for education and opened new schools, while overseas, missionary societies sent teachers and evangelists to every part of the empire.

In the Church of England, the Oxford Movement began in the 1830s as a protest against state interference in church appointments. It called the Church back to its divine origins and early sources, while repopularizing catholic expressions of worship discarded in the Reformation. It was both an academic and pastoral movement, scholars like Newman and Pusey writing learned tracts (hence the nickname Tractarians), Anglo-Catholic parish priests teaching a traditional faith through sermon and ritual, building ornate churches among the slums of industrial cities. The first religious orders since the dissolution of the monasteries were established in the Church of England.

✠

JOHN HENRY NEWMAN (1801–90) was an evangelical when he entered Oxford University in 1817. With friends there he began to recognize some ill effects of the Reformation and turned to a study of the early Church Fathers. Ordained in 1824, he became vicar of St Mary's, Oxford and used the pulpit powerfully to propagate the ideals of the Oxford Movement, published in *Parochial and Plain Sermons* (1834–42). He wanted to see a church more clearly in succession and continuity with the early centuries, but this quest led him to withdraw from the Church of England and he was received into the Catholic Church in 1845. In his *Essay on the Development of Christian Doctrine* he skilfully shows how seeds of theological ideas in the New Testament and early Church can come to fruition in later centuries. He was made a cardinal in 1879.

A Reading from John Henry Newman

For in truth we are not called once only, but many times; all through our life Christ is calling us. He called us first in Baptism; but afterwards also; whether we obey His voice or not, He graciously calls us still [. . .] He calls us on from grace to grace, and from holiness to holiness, while life is given us. Abraham was called from his home, Peter from his nets, Matthew from his office, Elisha from his farm, Nathaniel from his retreat; we are all in course of calling, on and on, from one thing to another, having no resting-place, but mounting towards our eternal rest, and obeying one command only to have another put upon us [. . .]

It were well if we understood this; but we are slow to master the great truth, that Christ is, as it were, walking among us, and by His hand, or eye, or voice, bidding us follow Him. We do not understand that His call is a thing which takes place now. We think it took place in the Apostles' days; but we do not believe in it, we do not look out for it in our own case [. . .]

What happens to us in providence is in all essential respects what His voice was to those whom He addressed when on earth: whether He commands us by a visible presence, or by a voice, or by our consciences, it matters not, so that we feel it to be a command. If it is a command, it may be obeyed or disobeyed [. . .]

And these Divine calls are commonly, from the nature of the case, sudden now, and as indefinite and obscure in their consequences as in former times [. . .] A man is going on as usual; he comes home one day, and finds a letter, or a message, or a person, whereby a sudden trial comes on him, which, if met religiously, will be the means of advancing him to a higher state of religious excellence, which at present he as little comprehends as the unspeakable words heard by St Paul in paradise [. . .]

Perhaps it may be the loss of some dear friend or relative through which the call comes to us; which shows us the vanity of things below, and prompts us to make God our sole stay. We through grace do so in a way we never did before; and in the course of years, when we look back on our life, we find that that sad event has brought us into a new state of faith and judgment, and that we are as though other men from what we were [. . .]

Or again, perhaps something occurs to force us to take a part for God or against Him [. . .] Some tempting offer is made us; or some reproach or discredit threatened us; or we have to determine and avow what is truth and what is error [. . .] That little deed, suddenly exacted of us, almost suddenly resolved on and executed, may be as though a gate into the second or third heaven – an entrance into a higher state of holiness, and into a truer view of things than we have hitherto taken.

Or again, we get acquainted with some one whom God employs to bring before us a number of truths which were closed on us before; and we but half understand them, and but half approve of them; and yet God seems to speak in them, and Scripture to confirm them. This is a case which not infrequently occurs, and it involves a call 'to follow on to know the Lord'.

Or again, we may be in the practice of reading Scripture carefully, and trying to serve God, and its sense may, as if suddenly, break upon us, in a way it never did before. Some thought may suggest itself to us which is the key to a great deal in Scripture, or which suggests a great many other thoughts. A new light may be thrown on the precepts of our Lord and His Apostles. We may be able to enter into the manner of life of the early Christians, as recorded in Scripture, which before was hidden from us, and into the simple maxims on which Scripture bases it. We may be led to understand that it is very different from the life which men lead now. Now knowledge is a call to action: an insight into the way of perfection is a call to perfection.

From *Parochial and Plain Sermons*, viii,
in E. Przywara (ed.), *The Heart of Newman* (Anthony Clarke,
Wheathampstead, 1963).

QUESTIONS TO PONDER

1. Newman is teaching here about the varied and sometimes surprising ways in which Christ calls us. The nineteenth century itself can be read in terms of God calling Christians to new endeavours and spiritual discoveries. Identify from our historical introduction the ways people found their vocation through the circumstances of a changing society. What message has this for today?

2. Newman urges us to listen out for the call of Christ in the daily occurrences of 'providence'. What is your experience of recognizing God's call through an everyday event, 'a letter, or a message, or a person'? How did it affect your life? How can we train ourselves to react with greater alertness to God's calls, and to welcome trials positively as opportunities for growth?

3. Newman teaches that even a bereavement can bring us 'into a new state of faith and judgement'. How can the experience of loss lead us into a deeper realization of God's grace?

4. Reflect on the amazing diversity of Christian callings. Look up Ephesians 4.11, 12, Romans 12.4–8 and 1 Corinthians 12.4–11. In his *Meditations and Devotions* Newman wrote, 'God has created me to do Him some definite service; He has committed some work to me which He has not committed to another.' How would you express your vocation and calling, as you understand it at present?

5. 'Now knowledge is a call to action: an insight into the way of perfection is a call to perfection.' How true do you feel this to be, as this course nears its end? Looking back over the Christian centuries, has any 'insight into the way of perfection' especially challenged and called you to deeper prayer or renewed commitment?

PRAYER EXERCISE

Either:

Reread the last paragraph of our extract about how God uses Scripture to teach us new things. Read slowly the call of Peter in Luke 5.1–11. Then go through the story again meditatively, imagining that you are Peter. Picture the details of the scene vividly in your mind. From Peter's standpoint, look at what happens and listen to what is said. What do you hear Christ saying to you? How do you find yourself reacting? Speak to Christ. What do you want to ask him? What commission is he giving you? What is he calling you to do for him? Conclude by thanking God for the way in which, in Newman's words, 'A new light may be thrown on the precepts of our Lord and His Apostles'.

Or:

Make a careful review of the previous day. Recall what things happened, whom you met (whether intended or 'accidentally'), what you did. Was Christ calling you in a way that you did not recognize at the time? Did you hear his voice – or miss it? Did you obey? Then take time to pray for a greater awareness of his presence today, and watch how God can bring people across your path and speak to you in unexpected ways and through unlikely individuals! Be ready to have your best-laid plans interrupted and stay open to God's surprises! Pray for a rediscovery of a sense of 'providence'.

FOR FURTHER READING

Chadwick, W. O., *Newman*. Oxford University Press, 1983.
Hughes, G. W., *God of Surprises*. Darton, Longman & Todd, London, 1985.
Newman, J. H., *Apologia Pro Vita Sua*. Fount, London, 1977.

The 20th Century:
Dietrich Bonhoeffer

THE TWENTIETH CENTURY, with its wars, changes and upheavals, has confronted the Church with the call to re-order its mission and rediscover its resources.

The marginalization of the Church through spreading secularism has heightened the need for a new evangelization. But with the necessity of finding appropriate ways to communicate the gospel verbally has come the urgency for Christians to share actively in struggles for liberation. Moving from 'prophetic' criticisms 'from above' of Communism and other repressions towards closer identification with victims of injustice, the Church has slowly developed a more holistic sense of mission, countering apartheid and other forms of racism, exploitation in Latin America, and playing its part in the fight against hunger and poverty in the Third World.

To underpin such a diverse mission the Church has needed to discover new and ancient sources of renewal. Since the founding of the World Council of Churches in 1948, ecumenism has led to a sharing of resources across traditions and to a deeper understanding of Orthodoxy in the West. The Second Vatican Council, called by John XXIII in 1962, depicted the Church as a pilgrim people, open to change, and led to worship in the native tongue and to a new generation of biblical scholars and teachers. Since the 1960s the Charismatic Movement has recalled Christians to a deeper awareness of the Holy Spirit. In places as diverse as Taizé in France and the base communities in Brazil (today's largest Catholic country), the idea of building Christian communities has re-emerged as a crucial priority in developing a credible and sustainable witness for today's churches.

Constantine's 'Christendom', where the Church was powerfully coterminous with the State, has gone for ever. There is perhaps a greater affinity with the pluralist age of the early centuries, the age of teachers and martyrs. Now is the age of the servant Church, fuelled by spiritualities old and ever new, a Church where everyone is called to be an apostle.

✠

DIETRICH BONHOEFFER (1906–45), Lutheran pastor and theologian, became a martyr of our times. After studies in Tübingen and New York, he was appointed a university lecturer in Berlin in 1931, and began a deep involvement in the ecumenical movement. Distressed to see the Lutheran and Reformed Churches becoming compromised in their subservience to Hilter's demands, in 1934 Bonhoeffer became a founder member of the 'Confessing Church', made up of German evangelicals prepared for resistance to Nazism. He headed a seminary for the Confessing Church at Finkenwalde, where he sought to form ordinands into a Christian community based on common prayer, study, confession and brotherhood. He expressed his vision for this in *Life Together*, while in *The Cost of Discipleship* (1937) he stressed the necessity for Christians' sacrificial commitment to Christ.

When his seminary was closed by the Nazis, Bonhoeffer accepted an invitation to teach in America, but at the outbreak of war he knew he had to return to Germany. He was soon banned by the Gestapo from public speaking, but managed to travel widely to support the German resistance movement under cover of a job with the Abwehr, the Government counter-espionage department. At this time he started to write his *Ethics*, in which he explored how Christians could make moral decisions in such a climate, within a conscience formed by Christ. He became convinced of the Christian imperative of Hitler's assassination, and got involved in such a conspiracy.

Gaoled in 1943 after helping smuggle Jews into Switzerland, he heartened those in underground opposition by letters later published as *Letters and Papers From Prison*. Aged thirty-nine, he was hanged by the Nazis in 1945 in the concentration camp at Flossenburg. In his essay 'After Ten Years', written in prison at the end of 1942, he seeks to make sense of history and reflects on the needs and challenges of the moment.

A Reading from Dietrich Bonhoeffer

Ten years is a long time in anyone's life. As time is the most valuable thing that we have, because it is the most irrevocable, the thought of any lost time troubles us whenever we look back. Time lost is time in which we have failed to live a full human life, gain experience, learn, create, enjoy, and suffer; it is time that has not been filled up, but left empty. These last years have certainly not been like that. Our losses have been great and immeasurable, but time has not been lost. It is true that the knowledge and experience that were gained, and of which one did not become conscious till later, are only abstractions of reality, of life actually lived. But just as the capacity to forget is a gift of grace, so memory, the recalling of lessons we have learnt, is also part of responsible living [. . .]

One may ask whether there have ever before in human history been people with so little ground under their feet – people to whom every available alternative seemed equally intolerable, repugnant, and futile, who looked beyond all these existing alternatives for the source of their strength so entirely in the past or in the future, and who yet, without being dreamers, were able to await the success of their cause so quietly and confidently. Or perhaps one should rather ask whether the responsible thinking people of any generation that stood at a turning-point in history did not feel much as we do, simply because something new was emerging that could not be seen in the existing alternatives [. . .]

Who stands fast? Only the man whose final standard is not his reason, his principles, his conscience, his freedom, or his virtue, but is ready to sacrifice all this when he is called to obedient and responsible action in faith and in exclusive allegiance to God – the responsible man, who tries to make his whole life an answer to the question and call of God. Where are these responsible people? [. . .]

I believe that God can and will bring good out of evil, even out of the greatest evil. For that purpose he needs men who make the best use of everything. I believe that God will give us all the strength we need to help us to resist in all time of distress. But he never gives it in advance, lest we should rely on ourselves and not on him alone. A faith such as this should allay all our fears for the future. I believe that even our mistakes and shortcomings are turned to good account, and that it is no harder for God to deal with them than with our supposedly good deeds. I believe that God is no timeless fate, but that he waits for and answers sincere prayers and responsible actions [. . .]

We have been silent witnesses of evil deeds; we have been drenched by many storms; we have learnt the arts of equivocation and pretence; experience has made us suspicious of others and kept us from being truthful and open; intolerable conflicts have worn us down and even made us cynical. Are we still of any use? What we shall need is not geniuses, or cynics, or misanthropes, or clever tacticians, but plain, honest, straightforward men. Will our inward power of resistance be strong enough, and our honesty with ourselves remorseless enough, for us to find our way back to simplicity and straightforwardness?

From 'After Ten Years',
in D. Bonhoeffer, *Letters and Papers from Prison*, revised and enlarged edn
(SCM, London, 1971).

QUESTIONS TO PONDER

1. 'But just as the capacity to forget is a gift of grace, so memory, the recalling of lessons we have learnt, is also part of responsible living.' As we approach the end of our journey through the centuries, what have been the most memorable parts? What have been the most helpful 'lessons we have learnt'? What mistakes of the past, regrettable episodes in the history of the Church, should be handled with penitence and 'the capacity to forget'?

2. What do you understand by Bonhoeffer's vivid phrase 'people with so little ground under their feet'? What insecurities do people face today? What is the source of our strength and hope? Recalling different periods in our journey through the centuries, how do you imagine that 'responsible thinking people of any generation that stood at a turning-point in history' might have felt?

3. 'Who stands fast?' Bonhoeffer expresses his concern for the sort of people needed in a time of great uncertainty. What sort of sacrifices do we need to make to respond as Christians to today's challenges? What sort of people do you think Christ is looking for today, who will lead churches into the future?

4. 'He waits for and answers sincere prayers and responsible actions.' If spirituality is indeed a 'combination of living and praying' how would you define the relationship between prayer and action? How does prayer enable risk-taking for the sake of the gospel? Bonhoeffer talks often of 'responsible people'. What should we be taking responsibility for?

5. Bonhoeffer calls his colleagues 'to find our way back to simplicity and straightforwardness'. In the light of the spiritual writers we have encountered, how would you say we can reach such a goal?

PRAYER EXERCISE

Either:

Take a newspaper and cut out pictures and headlines that express both suffering and hope. Lay them before a cross and pray that Christians today might find through the Holy Spirit the courage and generosity to respond aright. Read meditatively part of the Sermon on the Mount (so important to Bonhoeffer), especially the Beatitudes – Matthew 5.1–11. Close with an act of rededication to God, using the Lord's Prayer and the Grace.

Or:

Reread the fourth paragraph in our extract where Bonhoeffer presents a sort of *credo* or statement of belief. Compose your own 'creed' with four affirmations beginning 'I believe...'. Express your hopes for the future and your confidence in what God can do through lives of committed discipleship and prayer. Read out your affirmations in a spirit of rededication.

For Further Reading

Bethge, E., *Bonhoeffer: An Illustrated Biography.* Fount, London, 1979.
Bonhoeffer, D., *Life Together.* SCM, London, 1954.
Bosanquet, M., *Bonhoeffer: True Patriot.* Mowbrays, London, 1968.

Further Reading in Church History and Spirituality

T HE FOLLOWING RESOURCES have been invaluable in the preparation of this course and are commended for further reading.

Comby, J., *How to Read Church History. Vol. 1: From the Beginnings to the Fifteenth Century.* SCM, London, 1985.

Comby, J. and MacCulloch, D., *How to Read Church History. Vol. 2: From the Reformation to the Present Day.* SCM, London, 1989.

Downey, T. (ed.), *The History of Christianity.* Lion Publishing, Berkhamstead, 1977.

Jones, C., Wainwright, G. and Yarnold, E. (eds), *The Study of Spirituality.* SPCK, London, 1986.

MacCulloch, D., *Groundwork of Christian History.* Epworth, London, 1987.

McGrath, A. E., *Historical Theology: An Introduction to the History of Christian Thought.* Blackwell, Oxford, 1998.

See Also:

Chadwick, O. (ed.), *The Penguin History of the Church* (6 vols). Penguin, Harmondsworth, 1990.

Johnson, P., *A History of Christianity.* Pelican, London, 1976.

McManners, J., *The Oxford History of Christianity.* Oxford University Press, Oxford, 1990.

Acknowledgements

THE SCRIPTURE QUOTATIONS in this book are from the Revised Standard Version of the Bible © 1971 and 1952. Symbols at the start of each chapter are taken from W. Ellwood Post, *Saints, Signs and Symbols: A Concise Dictionary* (SPCK, London, 1962).

The author and publishers are grateful for permission to reprint extracts from the writings of the following authors:

Clement of Rome, Ignatius of Carthage, Anselm and Thomas à Kempis: used by permission of Penguin Books Ltd.

Cyprian of Carthage and Julian of Norwich: used by permission of Paulist Press Inc.

Basil the Great and Simeon the New Theologian: used by permission of St Vladimir's Seminary Press.

Augustine: used by permission of Oxford University Press.

Benedict: used by permission of Source Books.

Maximus the Confessor: used by permission of Faber and Faber Ltd.

'St Patrick's Breastplate': used by permission of SPCK and the Continuum Publishing Group.

Oengus the Culdee: used by permission of Darton, Longman and Todd Ltd, and Doubleday, a division of Random House, Inc.

Bernard of Clairvaux: used by permission of Hodder and Stoughton.

Teresa of Avila: used by permission of Sheed & Ward Ltd.

John Bunyan: used by permission of Kingsway Publications (formerly Victory Press).

Dietrich Bonhoeffer: used by permission of SCM Press and Simon & Schuster.

The publishers have made every effort to trace copyright holders. However, if any material has been incorrectly acknowledged, we would be pleased to correct this at the earliest opportunity.

The Society for Promoting Christian Knowledge (SPCK) has as its purpose three main tasks:

- **Communicating the Christian faith in its rich diversity**
- **Helping people to understand the Christian faith and to develop their personal faith**
- **Equipping Christians for mission and ministry**

SPCK Worldwide serves the Church through Christian literature and communication projects in over 100 countries. Special schemes also provide books for those training for ministry in many parts of the developing world. SPCK Worldwide's ministry involves Churches of many traditions. This worldwide service depends upon the generosity of others and all gifts are spent wholly on ministry programmes, without deductions.

SPCK Bookshops support the life of the Christian community by making available a full range of Christian literature and other resources, and by providing support to bookstalls and book agents throughout the UK. SPCK Bookshops' mail order department meets the needs of overseas customers and those unable to have access to local bookshops.

SPCK Publishing produces Christian books and resources, covering a wide range of inspirational, pastoral, practical and academic subjects. Authors are drawn from many different Christian traditions, and publications aim to meet the needs of a wide variety of readers in the UK and throughout the world.

The Society does not necessarily endorse the individual views contained in its publications, but hopes they stimulate readers to think about and further develop their Christian faith.

For further information about the Society, please write to:
SPCK, Holy Trinity Church, Marylebone Road,
London NW1 4DU, United Kingdom.
Telephone: 0171 387 5282